POLITICAL PROFILES
TED KENNEDY

Political Profiles
Ted Kennedy

Kerrily Sapet

MORGAN REYNOLDS

PUBLISHING

Greensboro, North Carolina

POLITICAL PROFILES

Barack Obama
Hillary Clinton
John McCain
Nancy Pelosi
Al Gore
Rudy Giuliani
Arnold Schwarzenegger
Ted Kennedy
Michelle Obama

POLITICAL PROFILES: TED KENNEDY

Copyright © 2009 By Kerrily Sapet

Library of Congress Cataloging-in-Publication Data

Sapet, Kerrily, 1972-
  Political profiles : Ted Kennedy / by Kerrily Sapet.
    p. cm. -- (Political profiles)
  Includes bibliographical references and index.
  ISBN-13: 978-1-59935-089-9
  ISBN-10: 1-59935-089-0
  1. Kennedy, Edward Moore, 1932---Juvenile literature. 2. Legislators-
-United States--Biography--Juvenile literature. 3. United States. Congress.
Senate--Biography--Juvenile literature. I. Title. II. Title: Ted Kennedy.
  E840.8.K35S27 2009
  973.92092--dc22
  [B]
                                        2008034943

Printed in the United States of America
First Edition

To my favorite Ted of all

Contents

Senator Ted Kennedy
(Courtesy of Mike Theiler/Getty Images)

one
The Youngest Kennedy

As a young boy growing up in New England, Edward Kennedy and his eight brothers and sisters discussed recent news events and carried on political debates during mealtimes. Thick slices of chocolate cake and glasses of cold milk often topped off their lively conversations. Although Edward sat at a table for the younger children, he soaked in the discussions, learning lessons about his country and the world beyond his large family.

These early dinner debates helped prepare Edward for his future in politics. Over the years, the Kennedys would become one of America's most famous political families. The public would avidly follow the lives of the family members as their triumphs and personal tragedies shaped the nation. Despite being the youngest child in the family, Edward would play his part, dedicating his life to serving his country.

Edward Moore Kennedy was born on February 22, 1932, exactly three hundred years after George Washington, in Bronxville, New York, just north of New York City. His parents, Joseph P. Kennedy and Rose Fitzgerald Kennedy, named the newest addition to their large family after Edward Moore, Joseph's longtime friend and assistant. Edward was the youngest of nine children. He had three brothers: seventeen-year-old Joe, fifteen-year-old John (nicknamed Jack), and six-year-old Robert (nicknamed Bobby). He also had five sisters: fourteen-year-old Rosemary, twelve-year-old Kathleen (nicknamed Kick), eleven-year-old Eunice, eight-year-old Patricia, and four-year-old Jean. Edward's family soon called him Teddy or Ted.

The Kennedys' ancestors had instilled the value of hard work. Ted's great grandfather, Patrick Kennedy, had first set foot on American soil in Boston, Massachusetts, in 1849, with nothing more than a suitcase tied with rope and hopes for a better life. Patrick had escaped a famine in Ireland, brought on by a disease that destroyed the country's main crop of potatoes. As many people in Ireland were dying of starvation, 2 million people fled the country. Despite American prejudice against immigrants, and the "No Irish Need Apply" signs that dotted windows preventing Irish people from applying for jobs, Patrick Kennedy quickly found work as a cooper (barrel-maker) and became involved in his community. His descendants proved no different.

Ted's father, Joseph Patrick Kennedy, was born in Boston in 1888 in a small wooden house, near the saloon his father ran. Joseph watched as his ambitious father soon became a successful politician, serving in the Massachusetts House of Representatives and the Massachusetts Senate. From a young age, Joseph too craved wealth and success. He earned money lighting streetlamps, peddling newspapers, and selling tickets for sightseeing boat tours.

As a teenager, while vacationing at the seashore in Maine, Joseph met Rose Fitzgerald. Slim, beautiful, and intelligent, Rose, like Joseph, had grown up around politics. Her father, John Fitzgerald, had served three terms in the U.S. House of Representatives, before becoming the mayor of Boston in 1910. A popular figure, people called him "Honey Fitz" because of his charm and beautiful singing voice. Joseph and Rose were drawn together by their similar backgrounds and ambitions. After Joseph graduated from Harvard, he and Rose married in 1914 and started their family.

Soon, Joseph became the youngest bank president in the United States. He made shrewd investments in the stock market, the real estate business, and the movie industry. It is also well known that he made a fortune as a bootlegger. Within ten years he was a multimillionaire. Joseph's wealth continued to grow, along with his family. He and Rose purchased a large mansion in Bronxville, a winter home in Palm Beach, Florida, and an eighteen-room summer house in Hyannis Port, Massachusetts.

Some of Ted's first memories were of the family's home in Hyannis Port. The town is nestled in the middle of Cape Cod, the hook-shaped peninsula that extends off of Massachusetts into the Atlantic Ocean. Ferries to Nantucket Island and Martha's Vineyard crisscross the salty blue waters of Nantucket Sound. Colorful sailboats glide across the waters and fishing boats wait in the harbor. Located on six acres of land, the Kennedy's large white clapboard house had wide front porches that offered sweeping views of the ocean. Here

Ted climbing a palm tree at the Kennedys' Florida home in 1941.
(Courtesy of Morgan Collection/Getty Images)

Ted, and his brothers and sisters, grew to love the sea and sailing. They played long games of football on the green lawns surrounding the house, frolicked in the cool ocean waves, and challenged each other on the tennis courts. Ted's brother Joe taught him to swim and sail, while John taught him to ride a bike and toss a football.

Occasionally, the older Kennedy children would torment their youngest brother, Ted. Joe, John, and Robert once talked Ted into diving off a rock twenty feet above the water, and they encouraged him to jump off the garage roof with a parachute. When Ted was six, Joe threw him off a sailboat into the Nantucket Sound for not knowing a sailing command. Joe dove in a moment later, though, to save his little brother.

With their father's encouragement, the Kennedy children tested themselves against each other in everything from sailing races to schoolwork to political debates. "We don't want any losers around here. In this family, we want winners," Joseph told his children, and they threw themselves into sports and debates to prove themselves the best. Despite their family competitions, though, the Kennedy brothers and sisters were fiercely loyal and quick to defend each other.

Ted's oldest sister Rosemary was born with mental disabilities. She still participated in most family activities, from attending dances to going sailing; though it was difficult, she was supported and helped by her siblings. Ted learned at an early age that people have different needs and that it was his responsibility to help those less fortunate than him.

With such a large family to care for, Ted's mother was a master organizer. She jotted down notes about her children on index cards, recording their shoe sizes, their recent illnesses, and other details. To maintain order, she imposed strict consequences for not following rules. Once, Ted received a brisk spanking for walking home from nursery school instead of waiting to be picked up, as he was told.

Instilling a strong religious faith in her children was especially important to Ted's mother. She emphasized learning about the Catholic faith and the Bible. The family attended church throughout the week and prayed every day. Rose mixed her religious lessons with stories about the Pilgrims and the Revolutionary War. Her children learned the importance of freedom, and about those who fought for the right to practice a certain religion or to win independence from another country.

The Kennedy family in 1935. Seated from left, Robert, Ted, Joseph Sr., Eunice, Rosemary, and Kathleen; standing from left, Joseph Jr., John, Rose, Jean, and Patricia. *(Courtesy of Bachrach/Getty Images)*

In the 1930s Ted's father Joseph became interested in politics, like his father and father-in-law. The year Ted was born Joseph had helped with Franklin Delano Roosevelt's presidential campaign, in hopes of being rewarded with a job in the government. Once elected, Roosevelt appointed Joseph chairman of the new Securities and Exchange Commission (SEC). Formed in the aftermath of the 1929 stock market crash when many people lost great sums of money because of shaky investments, the SEC monitored investments, provided people

Joseph Kennedy helped Franklin D. Roosevelt during his presidential campaigns in 1931 and 1936. *(Library of Congress)*

with reliable information, and made clear rules about dealing honestly with investors. In 1936, Joseph helped President Roosevelt win a second term in office. In return, Roosevelt appointed him as an ambassador to represent the United States in Great Britain.

The Kennedy family arrived in London, England, in March of 1938. They moved into the ambassador's residence, an elegant six-story building, at 14 Prince's Gate, where they lived like royalty in the thirty-six room mansion. Ted and Robert enjoyed running the house elevator and playing behind their new home in Ennismore Gardens, the largest private garden in England. The two rode bikes on the marble terrace and sailed boats in Hyde Park's S-shaped lake, called the Serpentine. They played a game with Princesses Elizabeth and Margaret—attaching messages to balloons, sending them into the air, and seeing who got responses from the farthest away. Sometimes, as a special treat, Ted went horseback riding with his father before school. Six-year-old Ted was a favorite with newspaper photographers: pictures of him walking his dog Sammy and petting a zebra at the zoo appeared frequently.

But life wasn't all fun and games. After the first few easy months, World War II steadily crept toward England. The war's roots stretched back to 1918 and the end of World War I when the victors treated Germany harshly, forcing the country to pay large penalties for causing the war. Discontentment with the treaty along with a devastated economy eventually led to the rise of Adolf Hitler, who had become the leader of Germany in 1933. Just five years later, German forces invaded the neighboring country of Austria. British and French leaders acted quickly to avert war. In the fall of 1938 they signed the Munich Agreement, which ceded certain areas of Czechoslovakia to Germany.

Adolf Hitler crushed any hopes for peace when German tanks, infantry, and aircraft invaded Poland on September 1, 1939. Great Britain and France quickly declared war on Germany. Soon, as Ted walked to school, he passed Londoners digging trenches and filling sandbags for protection against German bombs. Hundreds of barrage balloons floated above rooftops; the large balloons were tethered by metal cables, which would damage low-flying enemy aircraft upon collision. Ted, like the rest of his family, was fitted with a black rubber gas mask to help him breathe if poisonous gas bombs were dropped. He also was assigned to an air raid shelter. As the threat of war increased, he, his mother, and his brothers and sisters returned to the safety of their home in New York.

Although Ted's father stayed in London, he and Ted frequently wrote letters back and forth, in which Joseph described the increasingly desperate times. By May of 1940, German forces had invaded Denmark, Norway, Holland, Belgium, Luxembourg, and France. The *Luftwaffe*, the German air force, began launching heavy bombing attacks day and night on England. In one letter, Joseph described the ruins caused by the German bombs that rained down onto London.

"It is really terrible to think about, and all those poor women and children and homeless people down in the East End of London all seeing their places destroyed. I hope when you grow up you will dedicate your life to trying to work out plans to make people happy instead of making them miserable, as war does today."

Ted tucked his father's message away, remembering it for years to come. In the meantime, he began attending a new school. His mother enrolled him at Portsmouth Abbey School in Rhode Island, about sixty miles from home; she wanted Ted to attend the same boarding school as Robert. Portsmouth Abbey taught boys from the seventh grade up, but they accepted Ted, even though he was only eight years old. He was put in a special group with children from England whose parents had sent them to safety in the United States.

A scene of destruction in London caused by bombs from a Nazi air raid in 1940. *(Courtesy of AP Images)*

Young, immature, and somewhat overweight, Ted was an easy target for bullies. Annoyed at having to take care of his younger brother, Robert offered little help, telling his brother that Kennedys fought their own battles. The school lessons, planned for much older children, mystified Ted. After three miserable months at Portsmouth Abbey, he moved to a school closer to home.

Ted spent much of his childhood switching schools. After selling the house in Bronxville, the Kennedys lived in Palm Beach in the winter, and spent the rest of the year in Hyannis Port. Ted attended two different schools every year for fifth, sixth, and seventh grade.

As Ted battled his way through his education, World War II raged on in Europe. It soon touched the Kennedys again. Ted's father strongly believed that the United States should not become involved in the war, a deeply unpopular attitude in embattled Europe. When President Roosevelt was reelected for a third term in 1940, he ended Joseph's ambassadorship. Shortly after, Ted's brother Joe reported for military duty and became a Navy pilot. His brother John soon followed.

On December 7, 1941, Japan, an ally of Germany, launched a surprise air attack on the U.S. Navy fleet stationed in Pearl Harbor, Hawaii. The two-hour assault killed more than 2,000 Americans and wounded nearly one thousand more. It damaged and destroyed hundreds of planes and left twenty-one ships in flaming ruins. The events at Pearl Harbor plunged the United States into World War II. Four days after the attack, President Roosevelt declared war. The U.S. joined the Allied Powers, which included Great Britain, France, and the Soviet Union. They fought against the Axis Powers of Germany, Italy, and Japan.

The war dominated dinnertime conversation in the Kennedy household. Ted's parents expected him to take part in discussions, just like his older siblings. His mother sometimes pinned newspaper clippings to a bulletin board for him to read, then tested him on his reading. His father had him keep a daily diary, which Ted frequently turned over to be critiqued and examined for spelling mistakes. Ted quickly learned that to take part in family conversations he needed a topic to talk about, whether it was a detail from the day's newspaper article or an event at school.

Although Ted was the smallest child, his parents kept him from getting spoiled. They expected him to follow all of their stern family rules. If he arrived late for a meal, he missed whatever food had been served so far. Once when his father permitted him to take some candy to boarding school, Ted helped himself to two large boxes. Because of his greediness, Ted's father sent him back to school without any candy.

At eleven years old, Ted learned another important lesson. He and a friend took an overnight sailing trip and got caught in a storm. They spent the night on board being buffeted by the wind and rain. Exhausted, the boys rowed to shore the next morning. They called home and one of the Kennedys' servants picked them up. When Joe spotted his tired son trudging upstairs, he commanded him to finish what he had started. Ted went back to the sailboat and sailed it home.

That same year Ted's cousin Joe Gargan, who was close to Ted's age, came to live with the family. Joe's mother had passed away, and his father had died years earlier. Joe became a member of the Kennedy household. No longer the lone smallest child, Ted developed a close friendship with Joe.

Ted began enjoying his education more when he started attending Fessenden School, a boarding school in Boston. Although an average student, Ted loved to play football, and quickly became popular. He frequently got into trouble, though, such as when he and his friends tried to steal candy from a teacher. Ted looked forward to his weekends, as he often spent Sundays with his grandfather, "Honey Fitz." After the two had lunch together, they walked around Boston. Ted's grandfather showed him Boston Common, where British soldiers drilled during the Revolutionary War, and Park Street Church, where abolitionist William Lloyd Garrison called for the end of slavery. "Honey Fitz" made history come to life for Ted.

"He seemed to know every detail of the American Revolution, but what I remember most was his deep faith in the result of the revolution: the American dream," Ted said. "To him it meant equal opportunity, and opposition to prejudice wherever it existed."

During these years, Ted grew closer to his brothers. He and Robert sometimes traveled to the boarded-up family house in Hyannis Port during weekends in the winter. They stayed in the unheated garage, cooked food, and slept on cots. The two spent long hours together until Robert enlisted in the Navy in the fall of 1943.

Ted's brother John also made time for him. While in the Navy, he once snuck Ted onto a naval base so his little brother could see the torpedo boats. John had become an expert at handling the Navy's Patrol Torpedo or PT boats. The Navy used the fast, eighty-foot-long boats to attack larger ships.

By the winter of 1943, John was commanding a PT boat in the South Pacific, as the United States was battling Germany

John F. Kennedy aboard the PT-109 in 1943. *(Courtesy of John F. Kennedy Presidential Library and Museum)*

in Europe and Japan in the Pacific. As John patrolled the dangerous waters, a Japanese destroyer sliced his boat, PT-109, in half. Although John suffered an agonizing back injury, he guided his men to the floating remains of the boat. He helped them swim to an island three miles away, sometimes towing wounded men behind him. Afterwards, he swam to another island for help. His bravery made him a war hero. As John convalesced from his injuries at the U.S. Naval Hospital in Massachusetts, he sometimes read Ted stories about famous military and political heroes.

On August 2, 1944, tragedy struck the Kennedy family. During a dangerous bombing mission of a German submarine base, Ted's brother Joe was killed when his plane exploded over the English coast. The family learned of his death ten days later when two priests came to their home to break the news. For years, Ted's father couldn't speak of Joe without tears. Ted would remember Joe as always inspiring him to do better. Ted's brothers, Joe, John, and Robert, had each done their part in helping their country to defeat Germany. On May 7, 1945, German forces officially surrendered. Three months later, the United States dropped the first atomic bombs used in warfare on Japan. The bombs destroyed the Japanese cities of Hiroshima and Nagasaki. Japan soon surrendered, officially ending World War II.

In the fall of 1946, Ted entered Milton Academy, just south of Boston. He attended the school for four years, until twelfth grade, his longest uninterrupted span at any school. Ted bloomed at Milton Academy. He grew to six feet two inches, and filled out with muscle. He earned better grades and became more self-reliant. Although he struggled with learning Latin, he thrived on the debate team and in drama club. Ted loved stunts and pranks, and joined a group called the "Boogies" whose members performed antics like racing around the block in underwear. Ted's true love, though, was football. He practiced hard, learned fast, and was fiercely competitive.

"He would have tackled an express train to New York if you'd asked," said his coach. Ted also showed a talent for

The Kennedy Family in Hyannis Port, 1948. Left to right: John, Jean, Rose, Joseph Sr., Patricia, Robert, Eunice, and Ted (kneeling). *(Courtesy of John F. Kennedy Presidential Library and Museum)*

debate and public speaking. For years he had honed his skills around the Kennedy family dinner table. Now he was well-informed, poised, and good at articulating his views.

As the son of an ex-ambassador, and the brother of two war heroes, Ted had seen his family's pride in serving their country. He learned even more about the government when his brother John was elected to serve in the House of Representatives as a congressman from Massachusetts. After John won his seat, he often gave Ted walking tours of Washington, D.C., pointing out landmarks, such as the White House, the Capitol with the

American flag flying atop the dome, and the Supreme Court with its marble columns. Ted was fascinated.

"It's good that you're interested in seeing these buildings, Teddy," John said. "But I hope you also take an interest in what goes on inside them."

As Ted turned sixteen, two more tragedies touched the Kennedy family. On May 15, 1948, his sister Kathleen died in a plane crash as she flew over France. Around the same time, his sister Rosemary's disabilities worsened, and she began to behave erratically. She underwent a lobotomy, a surgery to sever nerves in her brain in hopes of controlling her mood swings. As a result of the operation, though, she became unable to care for herself. Her family placed her in a residential care setting as they could no longer meet all of her needs at home.

Despite the sorrows, Ted persevered along with the rest of the family. When he graduated from Milton Academy in 1950, he made plans to attend college in the fall. His brothers Joe, John, and Robert had all attended Harvard before him. The youngest Kennedy followed in his older brothers' footsteps.

two

Finding His Way

*I*n the fall of 1950, Ted Kennedy began attending Harvard in Cambridge, Massachusetts. Steeped in tradition, the university was established in 1636, sixteen years after the Pilgrims arrived in the United States. Legend has it that the school's first students heated their rooms by warming cannonballs in the fireplaces. For Kennedy, the school held its own family traditions. Like Robert and John, he worked hard to make the school's football team as a freshman, and lived in Winthrop House. Since this was the athletes' dorm, football games frequently broke out in the courtyard of the ivy-covered building. From Winthrop House, Kennedy had a good view of the Charles River, which separated Cambridge from Boston. As he attended his classes he often crossed the oldest area of the school—Harvard Yard, the large, shady, grassy park at the center of campus.

Kennedy quickly made friends on campus. At Harvard, like at his past schools, he enjoyed playing tricks and plotted his infamous Great Cairo Caper. He offered to pay for an airplane ticket to Cairo, Egypt, for his roommate, who then had to get back to the university on his own. Kennedy's roommate set off with a one-way ticket and a paper bag containing a toothbrush, a change of underwear, and a camera to prove he'd arrived in Cairo. At the last moment, though, Kennedy panicked and called off the stunt. He loved pranks, but he also was aware of the obligation he had to his family. Anything he did could damage the family's reputation and his brother's political career, including a newspaper headline about Senator John F. Kennedy's brother stranding his roommate in Egypt.

In the spring of 1951, Kennedy pushed his luck too far. When he struggled with a Spanish class, he grew worried that he would fail an important test. A friend took the test for him, and turned it in with Kennedy's name at the top. Realizing the student handing in the test wasn't Kennedy, the teacher caught them. Within an hour both Kennedy and his friend were expelled for cheating. University officials told them they couldn't reapply to the school for two years. At first Kennedy's father was livid, and then he calmed down and helped his son figure out what to do next. After a few weeks of considering his options, Kennedy decided to enlist in the Army for a two-year tour of duty. At the time, the United States was involved in the Korean War, which had begun a year earlier when North Korea invaded South Korea on June 25, 1950.

The Korean War was part of a period in history called the Cold War. After World War II, the United States and the Soviet Union had risen up as the world's two super powers.

The two countries clashed politically and economically, and soon became enemies. The United States is a democracy, in which citizens elect their representatives in government. The country also runs by the economic system called capitalism. Property, goods, and the means of producing them are mainly privately owned. People are free to own their own businesses and to make their own profits.

The Soviet Union was a communist country, in which the ruling Communist Party had control over political power, and industry and commerce were controlled by the government.

One of the principles of communism is that as the world evolves, more nations will become communistic. American leaders regarded this spread as a threat to democracy and the security of the United States. They believed in the domino theory that as one nation fell to communism the surrounding nations would also fall, like dominoes. American leaders and their World War II allies wanted a democratic world. People in the United States and the Soviet Union believed that the other country had plans to take over the world and their ways of life. Two events further fueled the fears of Americans. In 1949, the Soviet Union exploded its first successful atomic bomb, a technology only America had possessed before. Now it had the power to devastate cities around the world. China also became a communist country, renaming itself the People's Republic of China.

Over the next thirty years, each country would struggle to get more nations to adopt their beliefs. The battle would play out in different areas of the world. In 1950, the Cold War focused on Korea. At the end of World War II the United States and the Soviet Union had divided Korea in half. Both countries wanted to see Korea peacefully divided, so neither would lose any territory. Communist leader Kim II Sung ruled North Korea and democratic leader Syngman Chee ruled South Korea. Both men wanted to rule over a united Korea, and civil war broke out; North Korea soon invaded South Korea. The United States moved fast to contain the spread of communism, fearing South Korea would fall, while the Soviet Union and China supported North Korea. Soon war raged across Korea, with both sides gaining and then losing ground over the ensuing months.

As a soldier enlisted in the Army at the time, Kennedy began his basic training at Fort Dix in New Jersey. By January of 1952 he was stationed at Camp Gordon in Georgia for three months of military police training. Although he set a camp record for the number of pull-ups he could do, he also got into trouble. Once when he was supposed to be cleaning his rifle, he stayed out until after dark playing basketball. For punishment he had to clean the camp latrines.

Kennedy saw little of the ongoing war in Korea. In June of 1952, as both sides haggled over a truce, he was sent to Europe. Kennedy served as part of the honor guard at the North Atlantic Treaty Organization (NATO) headquarters in Brussels, Belgium. Formed in 1949, NATO is an international organization whose member countries pledge to settle their disputes peacefully and to defend each other against attack. As a NATO honor guard, Kennedy performed ceremonial duties and represented the U.S. military. On weekends he traveled around Europe. On one leave he climbed the steep Matterhorn peak, one of the most famous mountains in the Alps. On another adventure, he won a bobsled meet in Switzerland.

While serving in the honor guard for the NATO headquarters in Belgium, Kennedy was able to travel around Europe on the weekends. On one of these excursions he climbed the Matterhorn, a famous mountain in the Alps. *(Library of Congress)*

In March of 1953, after completing his service, Kennedy was discharged from the Army and he returned home. Within just a few months the United States and North Korea signed an armistice, or cease-fire agreement, bringing the Korean War to a close. Although nearly 300,000 Korean soldiers and more than 27,000 American soldiers had been killed, neither country gained much territory. By 1953, the line dividing North and South Korea remained much as it had been before the war began.

Back in the United States, Kennedy reapplied to Harvard and was permitted to return. That fall he worked hard in school and improved his grades. He also took time out of every week to travel into Boston to volunteer as a basketball coach for underprivileged children. While in the Army he saw that many of the enlisted men he worked with, especially African Americans, had faced tremendous disadvantages in their childhoods. Unlike Kennedy, they hadn't had the benefit of wealth, a strong education, and even certain civil rights and freedoms. Kennedy's military service had opened his eyes and exposed many injustices to him.

While he still played pranks at school, like making bets about hitting a golf ball across the Charles River and tying up a cow in a friend's room, he thrived in school. A course about the workings of the U.S. Constitution and the Founding Fathers fascinated him. He especially enjoyed the public speaking classes he took.

Football consumed him as well. One of his greatest moments at Harvard came on the football field. On November 19, 1955, in the middle of a snowstorm and in front of more than 50,000 spectators, Kennedy caught a pass and scored Harvard's only touchdown in a game against Yale. The two schools had an intense rivalry that dominated every sport and dated back to 1875. The competition culminated every year in the fall football game, which students simply called *The Game*. Though Harvard lost the game, Kennedy's family mobbed the locker room to congratulate him. His ability on the football field caught the attention of the head coach of the

Kennedy catching a football on the field at Harvard in 1955. *(Courtesy of AP Images)*

Green Bay Packers, who offered him a tryout with the team. Kennedy declined, though, saying he had plans to attend law school and go into the contact sport of politics, not football.

In 1956, Kennedy graduated from Harvard. For a short time, he worked as a reporter for the International News Service (INS) in northern Africa. His brothers John and Robert had also worked for the INS. The job gave Kennedy the opportunity to travel, to learn about politics, and to view events around the world. Soon Kennedy decided to attend law school. Like his brother Robert, he was accepted to the University of Virginia Law School. That fall, he started attending the school in Charlottesville, Virginia.

At school Kennedy quickly made a lifelong friend in John Tunney, son of the boxing champion Gene Tunney. The two lived in a three-room house a few miles from campus. They studied together for long hours under the high ceilings of the school library's reading room. Although Kennedy and Tunney worked hard, they also had fun. They threw plenty of parties, and Kennedy became infamous as a fast driver who racked up speeding tickets. As his number of speeding tickets grew, his mother asked him if he planned to be a lawyer or a criminal after graduating.

In Kennedy's second year of law school he met Joan Bennett, a beautiful, shy student at Manhattanville College of the Sacred Heart in New York. Kennedy's mother and sisters Jean and Eunice had also attended the college. Kennedy gave a speech at the college when his family donated money to build a new gym on campus. Joan had skipped the speech, but she attended the tea afterwards. Kennedy's sister Jean introduced him to Joan. Although she was four years younger than him, the two were attracted to each other. Joan had won beauty contests and modeled for television commercials. Kennedy also looked handsome, dressed in a gray suit.

Kennedy asked Joan out to lunch. The two continued to date that winter and into the spring. In June he invited her to the family house in Hyannis Port. There, they walked on the beach and played golf, and Joan, an accomplished pianist, played the piano. Joan also met Ted's mother Rose. The family took to calling her Joansie.

She had grown up in Bronxville, about a mile from the Kennedy's home. Although her family was not wealthy, Joan's father worked as a successful advertising executive in New York City. Unlike the Kennedys, Joan's parents, Harry and Virginia, rarely discussed politics. Joan and Kennedy had their differences too. She was shy, quiet, and not especially athletic, while he thrived on public speaking and competition. Still, she and Kennedy continued seeing each other.

Late in the summer of 1958, about a year after they met, Kennedy proposed to Joan as they walked along the beach in Hyannis Port. Joan accepted. Three months later, on November 29, 1958, the couple married at St. Joseph's Roman Catholic Church in Bronxville. Despite the blistering cold day, 475 guests attended the wedding. Ted's brother John was the best man. It was the first time Joan met the entire Kennedy clan. The ceremony marked the beginning of her new life, which in Kennedy's political family would be very public. After a three-day honeymoon in the Bahamas, the newly married couple returned to the University of Virginia. They rented an apartment and Kennedy resumed law classes. Joan took a few classes and, with the help of a few cookbooks, learned how to cook.

During his third year of law school, Kennedy became the president of the Student Legal Forum. His job was to bring important speakers to the university. With John's connections in Washington, Kennedy brought in several influential senators and Supreme Court Justice William Brennan. As Kennedy began to establish connections with

Kennedy and Joan cutting their wedding cake in 1958. *(Courtesy of AP Images/Jacob Harris)*

key Washington officials, he took another step closer to a career in politics.

One of Kennedy's crowning achievements at the University of Virginia was winning the school's moot court trials. A string of law debates simulating court cases made up the trials. Students argued about important Constitutional issues. In a trial about free speech, Kennedy and Tunney, as partners, won the competition. An effective debater, Kennedy could piece together tiny details and facts, creating a larger argument, in order to sway others to his point of view.

When Kennedy's oldest brother Joe had died, his father transferred his political hopes to his next oldest son, John. After serving for two terms in the House of Representatives, John had been elected to the Senate. Now, in 1958, he faced his senate reelection and planned to run for president in two years. Kennedy helped with John's reelection campaign, working tirelessly and seeing little of his wife. He traveled around Massachusetts, visiting factories, firehouses, diners, and schools, and talking about his brother. Once when he was stuck in traffic on a bridge, he got out of his car and began distributing bumper stickers.

By learning how to campaign, he was preparing himself for the day when he would run for political office. Joseph Kennedy dreamed of his three sons holding powerful positions in Washington, D.C. In 1957, the *Saturday Evening Post* had printed an article that predicted the career paths of the three Kennedy brothers.

"Fervent admirers of the Kennedys confidently look forward to the day when Jack [John] will be in the White House, Robert will serve in the Cabinet as attorney general and Teddy will be in the Senate from Massachusetts," the article said.

Robert Kennedy (left) conferring with Ted (center) and John F. Kennedy in 1959. *(Courtesy of AP Images)*

The brothers knew the plan. When John easily won reelection, Ted toasted him.

"Here's to 1960—*Mr. President*, if you can make it," Ted said.

"And here's to 1960—*Senator Kennedy*, if *you* can make it," John answered.

Shortly after receiving his law degree in 1959, Kennedy and his wife traveled to South America and spent the summer together. On their return, John's 1960 presidential campaign quickly consumed them. Kennedy became his brother's campaign manager in the western United States. Gone much of the time, he traveled around the country meeting with voters, handing out flyers, giving speeches, and filling in when John got laryngitis and couldn't speak. He also performed stunts, such as riding a bronco and hurtling off a ski jump, to attract attention to his brother's presidential run.

Ted and Joan Kennedy temporarily moved to San Francisco, California, to live closer to the states he hoped to help John win in November. During this time he and Joan celebrated the birth of their first child, Kara Anne Kennedy, on February 27, 1960. The couple still saw each other infrequently, though. One month after Kara was born, Joan also joined the campaign trail. She kept up a frantic schedule, shaking hands, meeting crowds, smiling, waving, and answering questions from the press. For shy Joan, unused to so much attention, campaigning proved to be difficult.

Many Americans saw John F. Kennedy and his popular, beautiful wife Jacqueline Bouvier Kennedy as glamorous figures. They captured people's imaginations with their charm and sophistication. Many people reacted to Ted and Robert the same way, as they too were part of the wealthy and intellectual Kennedy family.

On November 9, 1960, voters narrowly elected John F. Kennedy over Republican Richard Milhous Nixon, the former vice president. It was one of the closest elections in U.S. history. At forty-three years old, John F. Kennedy became the youngest president in American history.

On January 21, 1961, Ted Kennedy watched his brother get sworn in as the thirty-fifth president of the United States. Thousands of people converged on Washington, D.C., to see the inauguration. Kennedy stood in the Capitol plaza, shivering in the bitter January winds, and listening to John's first

Kennedy giving a speech during a campaign event for John in 1960.
(Courtesy of Ralph Crane/Time Life Pictures/Getty Images)

speech as the president of the United States. John's address would become famous, and often repeated to symbolize his years in the White House.

"Let every nation know, whether it wishes us well or ill, that we shall pay any price, bear any burden, meet any hardship, support any friend, oppose any foe to ensure the survival and success of liberty," he said. "And so, my fellow Americans: ask not what your country can do for you—ask what you can do for your country."

After listening to his brother's stirring speech, Ted and his family took part in the traditional inaugural ritual of the new president parading down Pennsylvania Avenue from the Capitol Building to the White House. Afterwards, they attended a tea at the White House. They ended the evening with dancing and dining at several inaugural balls. The Kennedys celebrated their day of triumph and gave thanks for their success.

By 1960, John had appointed Robert attorney general, and the prophesy of the three Kennedy brothers working in Washington, D.C., was two-thirds of the way fulfilled.

three
The Three Brothers

With John and Robert in the White House, it fell on Ted Kennedy to complete his father's goal by becoming the senator of Massachusetts. But after John was elected, Kennedy considered a different path. He and Joan talked about moving away from Massachusetts and settling in the West. They had enjoyed living in California when they worked on John's presidential campaign. In the West, Kennedy could practice law for a few years and then run for office. In a new and different part of the country, he would succeed or fail on his own, rather than achieving success solely because of his family name.

Joseph Kennedy had different plans. He wanted his youngest son to run for the Senate now, not later. Joseph persuaded him to move back east with Joan and their tiny daughter. In the loyal Kennedy family, it was Ted Kennedy's destiny to run for Massachusetts senator, and he couldn't shirk his duty.

In 1960, when John became president, he had to resign his seat in the Senate, although his term wasn't up yet. When a senator resigns before the end of a term, the governor of the state appoints a temporary replacement. In 1960, though, Ted Kennedy was only twenty-eight years old, too young to serve as the replacement senator (the law requires that senators be at least thirty). During the next statewide election in 1962, voters would elect a senator to serve out the remaining two years of John's term. By then, Kennedy would be old enough. In the meantime, the governor of Massachusetts appointed Benjamin Smith, one of John F. Kennedy's college friends.

Ted and Joan Kennedy moved into a spacious apartment in Boston. They also bought a slate-colored wooden house in Hyannis Port, near the home where Kennedy had spent his summers as a boy. The couple could look out the windows of their new house and see stunning views of Nantucket Sound. Kennedy began to work in Boston as an assistant district attorney, representing the government in cases prosecuting criminals. His days were packed, which left little time to spend with Joan and Kara. Although he worked as a lawyer, he had another job as well—laying the groundwork for his future senate campaign. When his workday in Boston ended at four in the afternoon, he traveled across the state, meeting people and giving speeches. He put in sixteen-hour days, as he readied himself and the people of Massachusetts for the 1962 senate election.

In Washington, in March of 1961, his brother John announced the formation of the Peace Corps. Through the Peace Corps, hundreds of men and women began to volunteer to serve in foreign countries. They worked with governments, schools, and other organizations to improve

John Kennedy greeting Peace Corps volunteers in 1961

agriculture, health, education, and more. Within just a few years more than 15,000 trained volunteers were helping people in struggling nations.

With the country's attention turned to the international community, Ted Kennedy arranged to travel to Africa with a group of three senators. He would accompany members of the Senate Foreign Relations Committee on a sixteen-nation tour of the continent. Later that summer he also traveled to Latin America, where he toured rural and depressed areas. The two trips expanded his background in international issues and his knowledge of foreign countries. His travels helped to build his credentials to serve as a senator and gave him material for his campaign speeches.

Both Ted and Joan Kennedy were busy. After a difficult pregnancy that required Joan to rest in bed, the couple's second child was born on September 26, 1961. They welcomed their new son, Edward M. Kennedy Jr. Despite the addition to his family, the new father still needed to focus on his political career. Ambitious and young, he continued to collect backers for his senate run.

Joseph Kennedy played a large role in helping to organize his son's campaign. A few days before Christmas, though, he began to feel faint while playing golf at a country club in Palm Beach. After he was driven home, a doctor visited the house and called an ambulance to take Joseph to the hospital. He had suffered a stroke, a blood clot blocking an artery to his brain. When blood flow to an area of the brain is interrupted, brain cells die and brain damage occurs. As Joseph clung to life, his three sons flew to Florida from Boston and Washington to be near their father. Although Joseph recovered, the stroke left him unable to walk, talk, or speak.

On March 11, 1962, Ted Kennedy made his national political debut on the television program *Meet the Press*. While John and Robert Kennedy could not officially be involved in their brother's campaign, they did give their little brother advice. Three nights before the television interview, Ted Kennedy visited John in the Oval Office of the White House. The president peppered his youngest brother with tough questions to prepare him for the interview. Although too nervous to watch the program that night, John called the interviewer the next day to find out how his brother had performed. In his first televised appearance, Kennedy made a good impression on voters.

Three days later, on March 14, 1962, Ted Kennedy officially announced his senate campaign. In the primary he would run against Eddie McCormack, the Massachusetts attorney general, who was a more experienced public servant. Both candidates vied for the nomination of the Democratic Party. The winning man would run in the November election.

The response to Kennedy's announcement was mixed. Some people were excited to vote for him because they had voted for John. Others felt differently. "One Kennedy is a triumph, two Kennedys at the same time are a miracle, but three could easily be regarded by many voters as an invasion," said journalist James Reston in the *New York Times*.

Kennedy's campaign provoked even angrier responses too. People argued he would only win the election because he was a member of the Kennedy family. Professor Mark De Wolfe Howe from Harvard Law School wrote:

> Teddy Kennedy seeks his Party's nomination for the Senate simply because he is the brother of the president. He knows as well as you and I know that were he not a coat-tail candidate his name would receive no consideration from any political body for such a high office as he seeks. His academic career is mediocre. His professional career is virtually non-existent. His candidacy is both preposterous and insulting.

Kennedy certainly did have an advantage because of his family. Not only had his two brothers forged a path to the White House, but he also had his family's wealth behind him. He had the ability to out-finance, out-organize, and out-work McCormack's campaign. Kennedy could afford to buy more television advertising time than McCormack, and with twenty offices in Boston and across the state, Kennedy's campaign workers papered the state with flyers. They mailed out 1.5 million letters and distributed thousands of leaflets by hand. They also made 300,000 phone calls to voters. Ted Kennedy flew across Massachusetts in a small plane, making nearly twenty campaign stops every day. He woke at five o'clock in the morning to meet workers at factory gates and campaigned late into the evening. He once even climbed a ladder to talk to a roofer in hopes of obtaining his vote in November.

Despite her two young children at home, Joan did her part. It was a close time in the couple's marriage as they worked together towards a common goal. Although campaigning was difficult for Joan, she stepped up to the challenge. She attended major public events, took interest in the campaign volunteers, shook hands with voters, and spoke in coffeehouses.

President Kennedy avidly followed the Senate race, despite a tense standoff with Fidel Castro, the communist leader of Cuba. Tensions arose when the Soviet Union began building missile bases on the island, located about one hundred miles off the coast of Florida. The U.S. threatened war if their aggressive actions didn't stop. Soon the two nations stood on the brink of nuclear war, but after two weeks the Soviet Union backed down. The conflict ended, although the United States would continue to impose sanctions on Cuba.

In the midst of the Cuban Missile Crisis, President Kennedy still had help to offer his brother. Although publicly he said that the campaign was his brother's race, he unofficially offered the powerful help of the White House. John's well-known speechwriter, Ted Sorensen, helped to write Ted Kennedy's campaign speeches.

The turning point in Ted Kennedy's campaign occurred in August of 1962 when he debated McCormack on television.

Kennedy walks through a crowd shaking hands during a campaign
event in 1962. *(Courtesy of AP Images/Frank C. Curtin)*

The two argued campaign issues in front of more than one thousand people in an auditorium in Boston. Uneasy and awkward, Kennedy gave a dull opening speech. He spoke incoherently and rambled in response to questions. In contrast, McCormack appeared at ease. He immediately attacked Kennedy's lack of experience and made frequent personal jabs. At the debate's end, Kennedy gave a composed closing speech, but McCormack finished with a thunderous, furious rant.

"I ask . . . if his name was Edward Moore, with his qualifications," McCormack said, then pointed his finger at Kennedy. "With your qualifications, Teddy, if it was Edward Moore, your candidacy would be a joke. But nobody's laughing, because his name is not Edward Moore! It's Edward Moore Kennedy!"

After McCormack's bold assault, the crowd and Kennedy sat in stunned silence. Then, the audience broke into wild applause, and McCormack walked off the stage like a prizefighter after a knockout. Soon the tide of public opinion turned against McCormack, though. Television viewers saw him as an aggressive, belligerent bully. In comparison to McCormack, Kennedy appeared to be a mild-mannered, restrained gentleman. With difficulty, he had controlled his temper and refused to acknowledge any of the attacks. Many also disliked the fact that McCormack had insulted the president's brother.

In the end, the debate gave Kennedy the edge over McCormack. Soon he held a substantial lead in the polls. On September 18 he received 69 percent of the vote, winning the Democratic nomination. Then, on November 6, he defeated George Cabot Lodge in the general election to become one of the two senators from Massachusetts. Joseph Kennedy stayed up late to watch his youngest son's campaign victory on television. Ted Kennedy called his father first when the victory was confirmed. Next he called his brother, the president of the United States.

On January 9, 1963, Ted Kennedy was sworn in to the Senate, becoming the youngest senator in a decade. Most senators averaged twice his age and had impressive backgrounds. Many of them thought voters elected him simply because of his last name. They knew little about him, beyond the fact that he was the president's brother. He needed to prove his abilities. Despite his back-row seat on the Senate floor, Kennedy had the benefit of getting advice from the Oval Office. President Kennedy advised him to keep his mouth shut, observe, and learn.

As a freshman senator, Ted Kennedy followed his brother's advice. He listened, sought advice, and respectfully introduced himself to each senator. He diligently went to meetings and studied key issues, often working late into the night. Most importantly, he observed how senators dealt with each other. He learned the rules of courtesy that took place on the Senate floor during debates. He discovered the tactics senators used to promote their causes and to help their bills become law.

As Ted Kennedy adapted to his new life as a senator, Joan Kennedy's life changed as well. They bought a traditional red-brick house in Georgetown; located in the northern part of Washington, D.C., the neighborhood was bordered by the wide Potomac River and had plenty of parks where their children could play. Joan stayed home with their young children during the day, and at night, after she put Kara and Edward to bed, she stayed up late, watching television and playing the piano, while she waited for her husband to return home. Quickly, she grew lonely and unhappy. While her husband thrived in the fast-paced social and political atmosphere of Washington, she did not.

In May of 1962, Joan suffered a miscarriage, adding to her depression. She began to turn to alcohol during her long evenings. As months wore on, her drinking problem worsened. She soon showed signs of becoming an alcoholic, as her mother had been. The following spring Joan suffered another miscarriage. Her mother-in-law Rose, and her sister-in-law Ethel, Robert's wife, had given birth to many children, while Joan had endured difficult pregnancies. Although she tried to follow in the Kennedy women's footsteps, she suffered from the physical and mental strain.

In the very public lives of the Kennedy family, Joan's troubles were kept quiet. She received little help dealing with her alcoholism. Despite her difficulties, there were happy moments, such as when she and Kennedy celebrated the birth of their third child, Patrick Joseph Kennedy, on June 14, 1963.

Away from his Georgetown home, Ted Kennedy learned about the problems affecting the United States. Racial tensions especially divided the country. Although the Civil War had ended nearly a century earlier, African Americans were still second-class citizens. They faced discrimination in many public places, such as schools, restaurants, movie theaters, hotels, and bathrooms. For many years the government condoned segregation in public places.

Kennedy had been in college when the U.S. Supreme Court had declared segregated schools to be unconstitutional in the landmark court case *Brown* v. *the Board of Education*. Before the court's decision in 1954, white and black students were required to attend different schools, but schools for African American children were often poorly equipped and overcrowded. The court decision had helped Kennedy see the power of government to instill change for good. It had sparked his interest in government and in the racial inequality that still blanketed the country.

Despite the landmark case, though, African Americans continued to face rampant discrimination, and for years, racial tensions had been increasing. African Americans protested across the South, demanding equal treatment and equal access to public places. Among other injustices in southern states, they were still required to sit in the backs of buses, refused service at lunch counters, and forced to drink water from fountains labeled *colored.* In 1955, an important demonstration took place in Montgomery, Alabama. It started when Rosa Parks, an African American woman, refused to sit in the back of the bus. Soon 50,000 African Americans across the city also protested by boycotting the buses until things changed. A year later the U.S. Supreme Court ruled to desegregate the buses. The peaceful and effective protests in Montgomery rocketed a civil rights leader, Dr. Martin Luther King Jr., to the forefront of the civil rights movement. King advocated nonviolent tactics to achieve change.

Demonstrations continued throughout the 1960s. In the fall of 1962, James Meredith became the first African American student admitted to the University of Mississippi. Although legally Meredith could attend the university, the governor of Mississippi, Ross Barnett, declared he would block him from attending the school "now and forevermore." Protests grew ugly when Meredith tried to register for classes. The

James Meredith, accompanied by two U.S. marshals, is jeered at
by white students after registering at the University of Mississippi.
(Courtesy of Francis Miller/Time Life Pictures/Getty Images)

Kennedys in the White House stepped in to protect Meredith's
rights. Attorney General Robert Kennedy reminded Governor
Barnett, "Governor, you are part of the United States." Barnett
responded, "I don't know whether we are or not."

John F. Kennedy sent four hundred U.S. marshals and
readied 31,000 soldiers to defend the one African American
student. Protesters hurled bricks, iron pipes, and bottles filled

President Kennedy speaking to the nation about civil rights in 1963.
(Courtesy of John F. Kennedy Presidential Library and Museum)

with flaming gasoline, killing two people and injuring many more. Although eventually Meredith was allowed to register for classes, the incident showed the ferocity of some people's opposition to desegregration.

Dr. King continued to push for nonviolent tactics—even in the face of escalating violence—and many African Americans followed his lead. In May of 1963 an incident in Birmingham, Alabama, drew more attention to King's peaceful, but determined, fight. Many Americans, both black and white, watched the television news in horror as police blasted peacefully demonstrating children with high-pressure fire hoses. Next they released police dogs on the protesters. Seeing the terrible violence on television changed many people's minds, and they began to support the civil rights movement.

On June 11, 1963, President Kennedy proposed a bill to abolish segregation, forbidding discrimination in public places. He promoted legislation that would require equal treatment of African Americans. Ted Kennedy worked to support his brother's civil rights legislation in the Senate.

Despite the racial crises rocking the nation, on Friday November 22, 1963, a shocking event shook the Kennedy family, the nation, and the world. As Ted Kennedy worked on the Senate floor, his brother John traveled in a motorcade in Dallas, Texas. People packed the streets to wave at the president and the First Lady. Then at 12:34 p.m., three shots rang out from the top of a textbook warehouse. Lee Harvey Oswald, an employee at the warehouse, had shot the president. Amidst horror and confusion, President Kennedy was rushed to the nearest hospital with critical injuries. The police quickly captured Oswald.

Hundreds of miles away in Washington, D.C., an aide ran into the Senate with the terrible news. Immediately, Ted left to try to contact his brother Robert, but he couldn't find a working phone. As thousands of people called to spread the tragic news, the city's telephone lines became overloaded, knocking out phones across Washington. After several attempts, Kennedy finally found a working phone. When he reached Robert, he discovered that John had already died from his injuries. Air Force One, the president's plane, would bring his body back from Texas that night. On the plane John's wife Jacqueline would witness the swearing in of Vice President Lyndon Baines Johnson as he became the new president of the United States.

Robert told Ted to call their mother, though they both worried how the news would impact their ailing father. Ted flew to Cape Cod, while Joan stayed behind with the children. Although Joseph knew something was wrong, Kennedy couldn't bear to break the news of John's assassination. He tore the television wires out of the wall, so his father wouldn't see the news on television. The next day he told his father, who was crushed to learn that he had outlived another child.

The following day Ted returned to Washington. Like millions of Americans, he watched another shocking event unfold on television. As officials transferred Lee Harvey Oswald from his cell in police headquarters to the county jail, a man named Jack Ruby shot him. Oswald later died of his wounds.

Across the country people mourned their slain leader. A very popular president, John F. Kennedy had appealed to many for his youth, energy, and liberal policies. His coffin lay in state in the rotunda of the Capitol building the night before his burial at Arlington National Cemetery. That night, as the light from the Capitol's dome lit the darkness, hundreds of thousands of people stood in line to pay their respects. Despite the freezing temperatures, they waited in a line that stretched for five miles to walk silently and solemnly past the president's casket. When Ted Kennedy walked in, the crowd parted to let him pass. He stood by his brother's casket with his head bowed.

Family and friends gathered for John's funeral service in St. Matthew's Cathedral in Washington. Underneath the ornate arched ceiling, prominent men and women, aides, and leaders from countries around the world joined the Kennedys in their grief. As John's casket was brought into the cathedral, trains stopped, traffic paused, and soldiers fired a twenty-one-gun salute.

The First Family watches John F. Kennedy's funeral procession in Washington on November 25, 1963. Jacqueline Kennedy (center), Caroline Kennedy (left), and John Jr. are accompanied by the late president's brothers Senator Ted Kennedy (left), and Attorney General Robert Kennedy. *(Courtesy of AP Images)*

The images from President Kennedy's funeral procession form some of the most famous in American history: the president's young son John saluted his father's coffin, a riderless black horse pranced down the street, and the two remaining Kennedy brothers walked down the street behind their brother's coffin.

As the nation grieved, controversy also swirled. People questioned whether Lee Harvey Oswald had been a lone gunman, or if others had been involved, such as the Russian secret police (KGB), the American Central Intelligence Agency (CIA), or the Federal Bureau of Investigation (FBI). Theories about the assassination spread and questions would abound for years. A special commission, led by Supreme Court Justice Earl Warren, would examine the assassination to resolve the questions. They eventually concluded that Lee Harvey Oswald had acted alone in assassinating the president, but to this day many people wonder if they heard the true story behind the president's assassination. Ted Kennedy would refuse to discuss any rumors or the findings of the Warren Commission.

After John's assassination, Ted and Robert Kennedy mourned differently. In his grief, Robert Kennedy retreated from the public eye. He and John had been inseparable, being close in age to each other and having worked closely together in the White House. Ted Kennedy dealt with his grief by involving himself in public commemoration ceremonies. He traveled the country on a tide of national mourning. He reminded people of John, and embodied the slain president's courage, charm, wit, and glamour. He traveled to Europe to raise money for the new John F. Kennedy Presidential Library and Museum. Near St. Patrick's Day, he traveled to Ireland, the Kennedy's ancestral home, where family ties ran deep. He spoke, as a senator and a family member, to saddened world leaders.

Ted Kennedy's message was sentimental, but it often turned political too. On April 6, 1964, he made his maiden speech on the Senate floor as he sought to help pass John's groundbreaking civil rights bill. Joan watched and wept, along with other onlookers, from the gallery as Kennedy eulogized his brother, in what many argue was one of his greatest speeches.

"A freshman senator should be seen and not heard; should learn and not teach. This is especially true when the Senate is engaged in a truly momentous debate," he began, but said that he was unable to sit by and not speak on this issue initiated by his brother.

Kennedy's voice broke as he remembered John. He called for the bill to pass. It would ban discrimination in employment, provide equal access to public places such as hotels and restaurants, and strengthen the prohibition of racist practices that prevented African Americans from voting.

"My brother was the first president of the United States to state publicly that segregation was morally wrong. His heart and soul are in this bill," he said in closing, as he urged senators to pass the bill. "If his life and death had a meaning, it was that we should not hate but love one another. We should use our powers not to create conditions of oppression that lead to violence, but conditions of freedom that lead to peace."

After Kennedy returned to his seat, senators one by one rose to congratulate him for his eloquent words. The Senate passed the historic bill on June 10, 1964. Abraham Lincoln had proposed the Emancipation Proclamation to free slaves, and President Kennedy's legislation was dubbed the second Emancipation Proclamation. Both presidents, though, were struck down by assassins before they saw the end of the oppression they fought against.

Although Ted Kennedy had achieved the passage of his brother's bill, tragedy soon struck again. In 1964 he launched his reelection campaign, and on June 19, he left Washington to fly to Springfield, Massachusetts, to receive the endorsement of the Democratic Party for the November election. The flight

President Lyndon Johnson signing the Civil Rights Act into law in 1964. After his brother's assassination, Kennedy championed the bill in the Senate. *(Courtesy of Lyndon B. Johnson Presidential Library and Museum)*

resembled many others he had taken. Often Kennedy raced to the airport for a late flight, took a long air trip, and landed in a small airport. But that night, fog and thunderstorms clouded the airport in Springfield where they were to land.

As the pilot attempted the landing, the small plane grazed the treetops and crashed into an apple orchard below. It somersaulted and hurtled for seventy yards. The pilot died instantly. Others within the plane suffered serious injuries. Kennedy's back was broken, along with several ribs, one of his lungs had collapsed, and he suffered internal bleeding. Indiana senator Birch Bayh and his wife, along with Ed Moss, Kennedy's assistant, had been traveling with Kennedy. Smelling fumes, Bayh pulled Kennedy, who was in shock, to safety. They were all rushed to the hospital, where Moss soon passed away. While the Bayhs had escaped serious injury, people feared Kennedy may not live. Gradually his condition stabilized, though. While he was temporarily unable to walk, he had not injured his spinal cord, which would have left him permanently paralyzed.

For the next five months Kennedy remained in the hospital. Because of his severe back injuries, doctors placed him in a large full-body metal frame to immobilize his back at all times so that it could heal. Doctors frequently turned the device to prevent bed sores and improve his circulation.

Although in pain, Kennedy kept busy. He began to paint.

Kennedy being moved to New England Baptist Hospital, Boston, from Cooley-Dickenson Hospital, Northampton, after being injured in a plane crash. *(Courtesy of AP Images)*

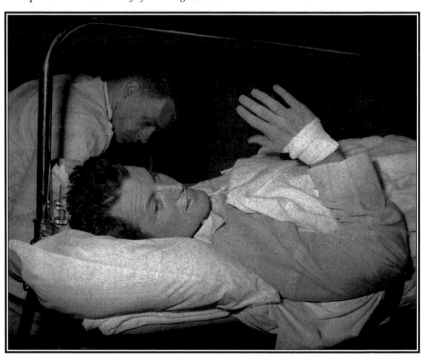

He also collected essays and memories about his father from family and friends, so that Joseph could be remembered as he was before his stroke. Kennedy compiled the essays into a book he titled *The Fruitful Bough,* similar to a book John had published when their brother Joe had died. During the day, Kennedy's children came to play and decorate his room with drawings. At night, he told them stories over the phone.

Kennedy also used the time to mold himself into a better senator. Professors from Harvard came to lecture him in economics, government, and science. They gave him reading lists and he began to study important and thorny issues.

"I never thought the time was lost," said Kennedy. "I tried to put my hours to good use. I had a lot of time to think about what was important and what was not and about what I wanted to do with my life. I think I gained something from those six months that will be valuable the rest of my life."

The accident, which occurred about six months after John's assassination, shook the Kennedy family. Rose Kennedy wondered if there was something about her family that incited violence. She pondered that maybe it was because they had so much good fortune. Maybe God didn't permit that much, she said. The plane crash also shocked Americans, who began to talk about a Kennedy curse. During Kennedy's first week in the hospital, they sent more than 40,000 letters and seven hundred telegrams. A steady stream of cakes, books, and fruit baskets followed.

In the wake of the accident, Kennedy never forgot he was in the middle of his senate reelection campaign. With her husband unable to campaign for himself, Joan stood in his stead. Over the next five months, she visited thirty-nine cities and 312 towns in Massachusetts, making an average of eight appearances each day. Joan's long days began early in the morning with a cup of coffee and a bowl of cold cereal. She gave speeches reporting on her husband's recuperation, talked about her visits to the hospital, and even showed family movies. With Joan's help, Ted Kennedy won a full six-year term in the Senate.

Other important events occurred in the November election. President Lyndon Johnson was reelected to serve a full four-year term as president. Robert Kennedy also was elected to the Senate; following John's assassination, Robert had resigned within a few months as U.S. attorney general, and moved to New York to run for the Senate.

In December 1964, Ted Kennedy took his first steps in six months. His spine had healed. His colleagues cheered when he returned to the Senate, leaning heavily on a cane. After the accident he had vowed to walk down the aisle of the Senate to be sworn in on January 4, 1965. He and Robert took the oath together, becoming the first pair of brothers to serve together at the same time in the Senate since 1803.

The Kennedys were together in Washington again, but other terrible events would soon follow.

four
The Last Brother

Ted Kennedy and his brothers often believed in the same causes. Although he promoted the same legislation, he also wanted to be recognized on his own, not just as the brother of the slain president or the former attorney general. During Kennedy's first senate speech, he had made a lasting impression when he argued for John's civil rights bill. Now again, he took up the cause of civil rights, but this time he would break new ground on his own.

In many southern states, African Americans faced discriminatory voting practices. Officials often required them to pay taxes at the polls and take literacy tests. White voters weren't subjected to the same requirements. These barriers prevented many African Americans from voting in elections. The poll tax was largely symbolic; no effort was made to collect it if the person did not try to vote. Although the new civil rights bill attempted to prevent discriminatory voting practices, it lacked the teeth to fix the problem. Martin Luther King Jr. began to lead almost daily protests to bring attention to the issue. Police broke up the peaceful demonstrators using whips, tear gas, cattle prods, and clubs. The violence rapidly escalated. White racists savagely beat a minister for eating in a restaurant in Selma, Alabama, that also served blacks.

On March 15, 1964, President Lyndon Johnson called for swift action in reforming discriminatory voting practices. He proposed legislation that would enable federal officials to register voters in the South, so that black and white Americans would have equal access to the polls and an equal right to vote.

"It is wrong—deadly wrong—to deny any of your fellow Americans the right to vote in this country," President Johnson told the nation in a televised speech. "There is no reason which can excuse the denial of that right. There is no Negro problem. There is no Southern problem. There is only an American problem."

Kennedy focused on pushing Johnson's legislation abolishing the poll tax through the Senate. In order to educate himself, he talked with legal authorities about voting rights laws and constitutional history. He even invited experts to brief him over dinner, a technique he used on many issues. Kennedy worked to retain the information so he could use it in a debate. Soon he was able to string together key facts about voting discrimination so that his arguments on the senate floor were informed, concise, and persuasive. He also brought publicity to the issue, because of his prominent family name.

Kennedy lobbied other senators to pass the bill. He made speeches, collected supporters, and even cornered his colleagues in the hallways to talk about the legislation. Although the House of Representatives passed the bill, Kennedy lost his battle when the majority of senators voted against the bill. Although he was defeated, Kennedy had gone a long way towards proving himself and becoming a leader in the Senate. He demonstrated that he could master a complex issue and lead a senate debate, bringing out small details to illustrate his argument.

Also, despite the defeat of the bill in the Senate, within a year the U.S. Supreme Court declared poll taxes unconstitutional, striking a powerful blow against oppression.

Over time, Ted Kennedy would help pass many measures that his brother John had initiated. He would become a leader in helping to ensure affordable health care for the elderly, improving access to college loans and scholarships, providing federal aid to schools, and establishing a National Teacher Corps of specially trained teachers to work in slums and poor rural areas.

Kennedy soon picked up another one of John's causes, attempting to end immigration discrimination. At that time, the U.S. immigration system provided a limited number of admission tickets to other countries. Each nation had a different quota of immigrants allowed to enter the United States. The laws allowed for 65,000 immigrants from Britain, but only one hundred immigrants from most Asian nations. Kennedy denounced the system, saying it discriminated against immigrants from certain countries. After giving stirring speeches on the Senate floor, a bill passed on September 22, 1965, ending the immigration quota system.

Soon Ted Kennedy turned his attention to Vietnam. In the 1950s the Cold War had shifted to Vietnam, a small country in Southeast Asia. Now the country was divided into a northern and southern state. North Vietnam, like North Korea, China, and the Soviet Union, was a communist country. South Vietnam was a democratic state. The North Vietnamese government wanted to unite the country, and the United States wanted to resist the worldwide spread of communism. They poured economic, military, and political aid into South Vietnam so it could defend itself against North Vietnam's strong military and stable government.

Ngo Dinh Diem, the leader of South Vietnam, had the full support of the United States. However, he proved to be a poor leader, ruling by fear, intimidation, and violence. The United States government, though, continued to support him because of his anti-communist position. His repressive regime and secret police forces caused the people to rise up in rebellion, and to resent the U.S. In the midst of the turmoil, North Vietnam worked to recruit supporters in the South. The Vietnamese Communists or VC organized rural peasants against Diem and terrorized the South Vietnamese army. As Diem's position collapsed, the U.S. government unofficially supported replacement leader General Duong Van Minh. In 1963, Diem was killed, three days before President Kennedy's assassination. President Johnson was left in control of an increasingly unstable situation.

South Vietnam's new leader, General Minh, proved even less capable of ruling. Coup after coup rocked the government and soon, despite massive amounts of American aid, South Vietnam was on the verge of total collapse and vulnerable to takeover. The United States had two choices: admit defeat or increase military involvement to protect the country.

U.S. helicopters depositing South Vietnamese troops in Vietnam in 1964. *(Courtesy of AP Images)*

President Johnson chose to attack. In January of 1964 he authorized secret hit-and-run raids on the coast of North Vietnam. U.S. warships patrolled the nearby waters of the Gulf of Tonkin and gathered intelligence to support the assaults. In August, one of the warships was attacked by torpedoes. Despite American warnings of retaliation, two days later the North Vietnamese soldiers attacked again. Johnson ordered immediate air strikes.

By the spring of 1965, U.S. Marines had moved into South Vietnam. At the time, many Americans backed President Johnson's involvement in the war, along with the use of soldiers in combat positions. Johnson began a bombing campaign that the military called Rolling Thunder to persuade North Vietnam to call off the fight in South Vietnam. However, many targets were off limits for the U.S. military as Johnson did not want to further provoke North Vietnam's powerful allies—China and the Soviet Union. They already were supplying weapons, and Johnson hoped to avoid a full-scale war with the two communist countries. Operation Rolling Thunder proved disastrous. It stiffened North Vietnamese resistance and killed 50,000 civilians.

In October of 1965, Ted Kennedy took a thirty-six hour flight to Saigon, the capital of South Vietnam. As a member of the Senate's Subcommittee on Refugees and Escapees, he wanted to investigate the war's impact on the country. As of 1965, nearly 400,000 Vietnamese had been driven from their villages by the war. As they fled the fighting, they crowded in city slums and refugee camps, where living conditions were poor. No U.S. policy existed to deal with the problem. The number of refugees would soon reach 1 million people. Kennedy saw that shortages of doctors, nurses, and supplies, coupled with government corruption, hampered U.S. relief efforts. He pressed Johnson's administration to do more.

Kennedy also focused his attention on health care problems at home in the United States. It was a cause with which he would distinguish himself for years in the Senate. His crusade began in Boston, with a new public housing project built for nearly 6,000 people. Although only four miles from a hospital, it took residents nearly five hours to get there and back by

Kennedy meeting with American and South Vietnamese officers in Vietnam in 1965. *(Courtesy of AP Images)*

bus and subway. Kennedy visited a medical clinic that doctors had opened near the housing project to solve the problem. He realized such clinics could provide inexpensive local health care to people in urban and rural settings. Kennedy pressed for the government to fund a program to develop community health centers. The $51 million he received was used to start thirty clinics. The program grew steadily, despite the increasing costs of America's involvement in Vietnam. By 1995, 850 health centers would serve nearly 9 million people.

Senator Kennedy also spoke out about gun control. He argued for a bill that would ban the shipment of weapons between states. John had been killed by a rifle that Lee Harvey Oswald obtained through the mail. When the bill passed, it banned only mail-order handguns, though Kennedy wanted to expand the legislation to ban other mail-order weapons. Although his attempts failed, he would continue fighting.

At home, Ted and Joan Kennedy's marriage began to grow increasingly rocky. The family had moved from Georgetown into a large home in McLean, Virginia, just outside of Washington, near Robert and Ethel Kennedy's house. Their new home overlooked the Potomac River, and featured thirteen bedrooms and a library. The move produced little happiness, though. Rumors spread that Ted Kennedy was having numerous affairs with different women. Unlike today, the media didn't focus as much on the private lives of politicians. Newspapers only dropped subtle hints about Kennedy's behavior and his marriage. The gossip reached Joan, though, who grew increasingly depressed and lonely. She began to drink more heavily.

Problems across the world in Vietnam also worsened as American involvement deepened. By 1967 nearly 500,000 U.S. soldiers were stationed in Vietnam, and 16,000 servicemen had been killed. American soldiers in Vietnam found themselves forced to fight in ways foreign to the U.S. military. Americans were used to fighting with traditional war tactics, such as direct combat. The side with the best soldiers, the best equipment, and the best generals became the victor. Not so in Vietnam. The North Vietnamese launched surprise attacks and had the advantage of being on familiar terrain. They ambushed the American and South Vietnamese forces, and then vanished into the thick jungle cover. They hid men and supplies in miles of tunnels that honeycombed the country. They used inventive weapons, such as pits filled with land mines or lined with sharpened bamboo sticks. They also used trip wires that sent thorny branches flying into the soldiers' faces. Their techniques kept the Americans in a tense state of constant alert.

As the need for more troops increased, the government initiated a draft, or mandatory military service. Under the system, all men eighteen years of age or older were required to register for a draft. They received a draft card, which listed their eligibility for service. If a man was listed as 1-A, it meant he would be required to serve in the military during the country's time of need. As more young men were drafted and sent to fight in Vietnam, opposition to the war increased in the United States. Students on college campuses began to protest. Some men illegally burned their draft cards or tried to fail their military physicals. Others avoided compulsory military service by moving to Canada. By doing so, they broke the law, and could be imprisoned if they returned to the United States.

Soldiers, even those who were drafted, faced criticism from protesters. Angry protesters often yelled insults and threw things at soldiers in uniform. Those who refused to serve also faced criticism from the war's supporters. The war in Vietnam quickly divided the country like no war had since the Civil War.

As more men were drafted into service, Kennedy fought to make the system fairer, even though he disagreed with American involvement in Vietnam. At that time, men could avoid the draft if they were fathers, college students, or employed in certain occupations. Kennedy argued that these deferments discriminated against younger, poorer,

Kennedy giving a speech in 1967, during which he advocated reforms in the selective service system. *(Courtesy of AP Images)*

and less-educated men. He pushed for a random lottery system that was fair to all. In 1968 he introduced legislation calling for broad draft reform. Although his bill stalled, a bill later passed that included many of his proposed reforms.

In January of 1968, Kennedy returned to Vietnam for a two-week-long fact-finding mission. Although under constant bomb threats, he examined hospitals and refugee camps and talked to experts. Back in the U.S., Kennedy increased pressure for better medical care for wounded soldiers. He also renewed his emphasis on Vietnamese refugees, as they now were fleeing U.S. military efforts as well. Herbicides, such as

Agent Orange, that the military used to kill the jungle cover that camouflaged the enemy, also killed crops, leaving civilians without food. Soldiers also used napalm, a sticky, gel-like, flammable substance. When dropped, napalm ignited, causing an inferno that demolished everything in its path. It destroyed not only the enemy, but civilians, friendly troops, and the surrounding countryside.

Kennedy supported a new report written by American doctors who called for better medical care, more medics, and more supplies. When the administration released the doctors' report, key portions were kept secret, leaving Kennedy furious. His visit only served to reinforce his opinion. Like many Americans, he had decided that the war was a disaster.

On January 31, 1968, American opinion of the war sank even lower. On the Vietnamese holiday called Tet, when many South Vietnamese soldiers were on leave, 85,000 North Vietnamese forces launched a coordinated surprise attack. They struck one hundred cities and towns across South Vietnam. Although the Tet Offensive gained little ground, the political implications of the attacks were disastrous in the United States.

The Vietnam War was the first major conflict to be shown to all Americans via television news. Many Americans saw the graphic effects of the Tet Offensive on television. People saw bombed villages, dead and wounded soldiers, and frightened civilians. The media coverage differed from the picture President Johnson painted—that the war efforts were proving to be a success, and the conflict would soon end. The TV coverage proved to the American people that the communists were not on the run. The United States was not winning the war, and American soldiers were dying at alarming rates.

American leaders lost the little remaining support they had for the war. People argued that the government had no clear plan to end the war.

After the Tet Offensive, Kennedy's brother Robert struggled to make a difficult decision. Long a fierce opponent of President Johnson's policies, he had condemned Johnson's refusal to negotiate with North Vietnam to try to end the conflict. Because of Robert's opinions, many wondered if he would run against Johnson for president in the upcoming 1968 election. At first Robert refused, although his supporters urged him to run.

Ted Kennedy opposed his brother running for president for several reasons. He questioned whether Robert would be able to defeat Johnson in the primaries. If Robert lost the election, it would hurt his chances of winning a presidential election in 1972. Privately, Kennedy also feared that his brother would be assassinated like John.

Robert Kennedy had the same reservations. However, he ultimately decided to run for president because of his strong convictions about the war and many other issues, such as civil rights. On March 16, 1968, he officially announced he was running for president, saying he felt obligated to run.

"I have such strong feelings about what must be done," Robert said. He wanted to initiate new policies that would "end the bloodshed in Vietnam and in our cities, policies to close the gap that now exists between black and white, rich and poor, between young men and old in this country and around the world."

Then, in a surprise announcement on March 31, President Johnson announced that he would not run for reelection. Due to the Vietnam War, Johnson's popularity had plummeted.

Kennedy (center) arriving to attend funeral services for Dr. Martin Luther King Jr. after King's assassination in 1968. *(Courtesy of AP Images/ Jack Thornell)*

Robert Kennedy suddenly became a serious contender for the Democratic nomination. It was becoming apparent that his opponent would probably be Richard Milhouse Nixon, a former senator from California who had served as President Dwight D. Eisenhower's vice president. Nixon had previously run for president in 1960, but had been beaten by John Kennedy.

Four days later, on April 4, 1968, another assassination rocked the country. Martin Luther King had been planning a demonstration in Memphis, Tennessee. As he stood on the balcony of his motel, calling to Jesse Jackson, a fellow organizer, Dr. King was shot by a white racist named James Earl Ray. In the aftermath of King's assassination, widespread riots broke out all over the country.

Robert Kennedy was one of the calm voices on April 4. At a campaign speech in Indianapolis, Indiana, he gave what many call his greatest speech as he faced a primarily black audience. He brought them the news of King's assassination. At a moment when tensions between whites and blacks were at their zenith, he gave a speech that bridged the gap between the races, if only for that moment, as he advocated for calm and kindness. "Let us dedicate ourselves to what the Greeks wrote so many years ago: to tame the savageness of man and make gentle the life of this world," he said. While rioting continued across the country into the night, Indianapolis remained calm and riot-free.

In Colorado, Ted Kennedy, who was campaigning for his brother Robert, referenced King's famous "I Have a Dream" speech made at Lincoln Memorial in Washington, D.C.

"He will never see that dream," Ted Kennedy said, "but the moment we realize his dream is our dream and work to make it ours, the nation can survive."

Despite his reservations about his brother running, Kennedy devoted himself to Robert's presidential race. The two talked by phone or in person nearly every day. Often the best time to talk was when Robert was relaxing in a hot tub after a long, hard day of campaigning.

When the primary races began, Robert immediately claimed victories. A critical primary occurred in California on June 5. Robert remained in Los Angeles, as results came in, while Ted stayed in San Francisco. By the end of the night, Robert had won the primary in California. He gave his victory speech in a crowded hotel ballroom, packed with supporters. Robert and his aides took a shortcut through the hotel's kitchen to leave. Lying in wait in the kitchen was Sirhan Bishara Sirhan, an Arab immigrant who was outraged at Robert Kennedy's support of Israel. Sirhan viewed Kennedy

Robert Kennedy speaking to campaign workers at the Ambassador Hotel in Los Angeles, California. Just moments after this speech, Kennedy was shot and killed by Sirhan Bishara Sirhan as he walked through the hotel's kitchen. *(Courtesy of AP Images)*

as an enemy of all Arab people. He shot Kennedy three times at point blank range. Seriously injured, Robert Kennedy was rushed to the hospital.

Ted Kennedy heard the news of his brother's shooting on television and immediately flew to Los Angeles. Although doctors operated on Robert, he had lost a critical amount of blood to his brain. On June 6, the following morning, he died. Ted Kennedy's fears had come true.

Frank Mankiewicz, a press secretary, saw Kennedy at the hospital, "sort of leaning over the sink with the most awful expression on his face," he said. "Just more than agony, more than anguish. I don't know if there is a word for it."

Only one hour later Robert Kennedy's supporters pressed a devastated Ted Kennedy to complete his brother's presidential race. Kennedy could barely contain his grief, much less pick up where Robert had left off. Robert had been his only remaining brother. The nearest in age and a fellow senator, the two had shared a close relationship. For five years, the two younger Kennedys had planned and acted together. They had stood together in times of victory and in times of sorrow, such as when John had been assassinated five years earlier.

During the funeral mass at St. Patrick's Cathedral, in New York, friends feared that Ted Kennedy would be unable to deliver a eulogy for his brother, without being overcome by grief. He did deliver an eloquent speech, remembering his brother as, "a good and decent man who saw wrong and tried to right it, saw suffering and tried to heal it, saw war and tried to stop it." He then quoted one of his brother's favorite lines:

"As he said many times, in many parts of this nation, to those he touched and who sought to touch him: Some men see things as they are and say why. I dream things that never were, and say why not."

Ted Kennedy traveled on the funeral train that took Robert's coffin and his mourners south, back to Washington, D.C., for burial in Arlington Cemetery next to John. Tearful crowds lined the railroad tracks. While Ted remained in the railroad car with the casket, Robert's wife Ethel and oldest son, Joseph P. Kennedy II, walked through the train,

Kennedy eulogizing his brother Robert at his funeral in 1968. *(Courtesy of AP Images)*

thanking the mourners. When they arrived in Washington, D.C., at night, a solemn crowd met the train. In the darkness, mourners held candles that lit the night. Robert Kennedy was buried on June 8, 1968.

With Robert's burial, Ted Kennedy became the last survivor of the four Kennedy brothers. His brothers Joe, John, and Robert all had died in the service of their country. With his elderly father incapacitated by his stroke, Ted Kennedy stood at the head of the large Kennedy family. It was a weighty public and private responsibility.

In the wake of the crushing blow of his brother's assassination, Ted Kennedy withdrew from the public eye for the rest of the year. He and Joan also saw little of each other. She alone had told their children about their Uncle Robert's death. Ted Kennedy retreated from his life. He escaped to the sea, sailing up and down the coast of Maine. He took little care of himself and grew a wild beard. Sad rumors circulated that he had begun drinking heavily. He had little interest in his career and at times considered withdrawing from politics altogether. Kennedy talked about buying a newspaper company or running a sailboat charter business. He tried to return to the Senate in mid-July, but found himself unable to get out of the car.

Although Ted Kennedy was unable to face his political life at the time, people speculated that he might run as a vice-presidential candidate with Hubert Humphrey in 1968. At the end of July, he issued a statement to put the rumors to an end.

"Over the last few weeks, many prominent Democrats have raised the possibility of my running for vice president on the Democratic ticket this fall," he wrote. "I deeply appreciate their confidence. Under normal circumstances, such a possibility would be a high honor and a challenge to further public service. But for me, this year, it is impossible."

The world of politics pressed on, drawing attention away from Kennedy. In August, as expected, Republicans nominated Richard Nixon as their candidate. Later that month, Hubert Humphrey accepted the nomination of the Democratic Party. Kennedy called Humphrey to congratulate him, and then he forced himself back into the public eye to carry on Robert's fight against the war and for civil rights. In a nationally televised speech he announced that he would not retire, despite the dangers associated with politics.

"Like my brothers before me," he said. "I pick up a fallen standard. Sustained by the memory of our priceless years together, I shall try to carry forward that special commitment to justice, to excellence, and to courage that distinguished their lives." He added, "There is no safety in hiding."

Kennedy continued to speak out sharply against the war. He advocated a halt to the bombing, a decrease in troops, and a renewal of peace talks, but he remained uninvolved in the 1968 presidential campaign.

Life moved forward both privately and publicly. On October 20, 1968, John Kennedy's widow Jackie married Greek shipping billionaire Aristotle Onassis on the island of Skorpios. In November, Richard Nixon, who promised to get tough on communism and bring soldiers home, won the election and became the next president of the United States.

In December 1968, Ted Kennedy made a decision that surprised many. He decided to run for the position of Deputy Majority Leader, or Whip, in the Senate. It was the Whip's duty to learn how each member of his party would vote on important pieces of legislation and to help bring them all into line to achieve party unity. Supported by his fellow senators, Kennedy won the position. Many thought the decision had political implications and meant that Kennedy planned to run for president in 1972. Someone even scratched the words *Mr. President* into the wood of his desk.

By 1969, Ted Kennedy had been a senator for six years. He enjoyed the ways of the Senate and had an easy rapport with older senators. His accomplishments included the passage of a key civil rights bill, the elimination of poll taxes and immigration quotas, and legislation that established community health centers and a teacher corps. Kennedy also renewed his battle for stricter gun control laws. In the wake of Robert's assassination, Congress actively picked up the fight, amidst a flood of criticism and attention over lax gun laws. They extended the ban on mail-order weapons to include long guns. Over the years, the fight would continue, often spearheaded by Kennedy. Today gun-control laws require all gun owners to obtain a license and to register their guns.

Privately, Kennedy focused his attention on caring for his fatherless nieces and nephews. Robert's death had left his eleven children without a father, and John's death two. Concerned about the children, Ted Kennedy often played with them and offered them advice. He took Robert's oldest daughter Kathleen with him sometimes when he gave speeches about her father. He helped connect his nieces and nephews with their absent fathers.

Although life continued, Washington, D.C., would always remain a place of memories of his brothers.

"I like to walk whenever I can and go by where both Jack's [John's] office was and where Bobby's office was," he said. "I can remember different things Bobby said as I pass by the places where we stood and talked. When I go by the north entrance hall [of the Capitol building], I think of President Kennedy delivering his inaugural address there and I remember that was where the country honored him at the end."

five
Scandal and Sorrow

Although Kennedy had decided to continue serving in the Senate, the loss of his brothers haunted him. Memories ran deep and listening to friends and colleagues speak of John and Robert was difficult.

Still, he carried on, but in July of 1969, an accident occurred, sparked by a party with some of Robert's campaign workers. The incident would forever change Kennedy's life. It began with a swim, a sailing race, and a plate of fried clams.

On July 18, 1969, Kennedy flew to the island of Martha's Vineyard in Cape Cod. He planned to race John's sailboat *Victura* in a regatta he competed in each year. Before the competition, Kennedy stopped off for some fried clams and a cool refreshing swim. After finishing ninth in the sailing race, he planned to attend a party with friends, including six women who had worked on Robert's campaign. The party would be held in a small cottage on Chappaquiddick Island, a

tiny community sep-
arated from Martha's
Vineyard and the vil-
lage of Edgartown by
a seawater channel.

That evening, as
the night wore on,
partygoers remi-
nisced about Robert.
When Mary Joe
Kopechne, a sec-
retary in Robert's
senate office, said
she didn't feel well,
Kennedy offered to
take her back to her
motel. They drove
onto the island's unlit
road, and turned onto
the narrow bridge
crossing the chan-
nel. But the bridge

Mary Joe Kopechne *(Courtesy of AP Images)*

was built at an odd angle, and had no guardrails. In the dark,
Kennedy could not see where he was going, and the car
plunged off the edge into the water. His car overturned and
immediately filled with water.

Kennedy struggled to the surface. He made repeated dives
back toward the car, but he was unable to rescue Kopechne in
the dark, murky water. He returned to the party and asked his
cousin Joe Gargan and his friend Paul Markham to help him
save Kopechne. Not wanting to alert and possibly endanger

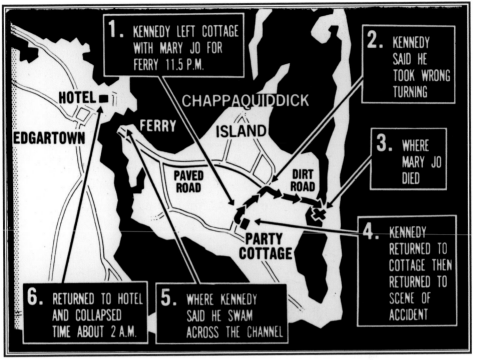

A map detailing the location of events of July 18, 1969, on Chappaquiddick Island. *(Courtesy of Express Newspapers/Getty Images)*

the other partygoers, who were close friends of Kopechne's, the three men headed to the bridge, but the water's strong currents prevented them from rescuing her. Kennedy assured his friends he would alert the authorities, then swam back to Edgartown and returned to his hotel, where he quickly fell asleep.

The following morning, at about 8 a.m., Gargan and Markham visited Kennedy's room. They pointedly asked why he hadn't yet reported the incident. Kennedy responded that during the night he had been hoping that the next morning they would arrive and report that Kopechne had escaped. He also claimed to have been in shock.

Meanwhile, two amateur fishermen spotted the over-turned car in the water. They promptly called the authorities, at around 8:20 a.m. By 8:45, police were on the scene, and a police diver discovered Kopechne, drowned in the car. At about 9:45 am, Kennedy went to the Edgartown police station and reported the accident.

News of the accident spread fast, along with rumors about the evening. People gossiped about the married senator, the attractive Kopechne, and the evening beach party. Ted Kennedy had a reputation for having affairs with other women. People wondered if he had been trying to evade the law by leaving the scene of the accident and not notifying authorities until the morning. They questioned whether he and Kopechne had been drinking, and whether he had caused the accident by driving under the influence of alcohol.

Ted Kennedy attended Mary Joe Kopechne's funeral, and on July 25 made a public statement to address the rumors. Television viewers watched and listened as Kennedy explained his actions that evening. He acknowledged his irresponsibility in leaving the scene of the accident. The impact of the car hitting the water had given Kennedy a mild concussion, which often results in impaired judgment, but Kennedy said that was no excuse for the loss of Kopechne's life.

"I was overcome, I'm frank to say," he said, "by a jumble of emotions, grief, fear, doubt, exhaustion, panic, confusion, and shock."

He asked the people of Massachusetts to determine his fate. If they decided he could no longer work effectively as their senator, he would retire from public life. Within days an avalanche of letters and telegrams arrived supporting him. But the wave of public support soon faded, along with the early burst of sympathy for the rumors Senator Kennedy endured. More people started to question his account of events. His office began to receive hate mail.

In a trial, he pleaded guilty to leaving the scene of the accident, but not to charges of manslaughter. He was sentenced to two months incarceration but his sentence was suspended, though he did lose his driver's license for one year. For years after, people speculated about the incident. Did something more happen than Kennedy let on? Some even speculated that the incident was a conspiracy organized to keep Kennedy from running for president in 1972.

The accident at Chappaquiddick impacted Joan too. As people gossiped about her husband's behavior and their marriage, she did not appear with her husband in public. Although the Kennedy family remained secluded at Hyannis Port that August, Joan's health worsened. In her depression, she continued to turn to alcohol.

Under the strain, Ted Kennedy lost weight and told friends he had lost his zeal for politics. However, he announced that he would remain in the Senate. When Kennedy returned to Washington, he received much media attention. Although his colleagues welcomed him back, his standing in the Senate had diminished. Many people now questioned his judgment. He once again threw himself into his work. He focused on introducing measures that would make health insurance coverage affordable for everyone.

However, Kennedy's influence in Washington, D.C., had suffered because of the Chappaquiddick scandal. His staff became integral to his ability to effect change. He gave them more responsibility, empowered them, and listened

Kennedy discussing health care in 1971. *(Courtesy of AP Images)*

to their suggestions and advice. Aides in his office often stayed longer than assistants in most offices. They worked hard, and in return Kennedy kept his top aides by supplementing their salaries with his own personal funds. Throughout the years, Kennedy's staff would play an important role in helping him pass legislation.

In September, he turned his attention to Vietnam. He had spoken out many times against the war, criticizing the lack of refugee programs and denouncing specific battles. Now he sharpened his criticism. Although President Nixon had begun to slowly withdraw troops, Kennedy called for him to bring the troops home faster, as the violence in Vietnam had not decreased. In 1969, 9,000 American soldiers died. Many soldiers in Vietnam decided they were waging an unwinnable war, and troop morale worsened as the war continued. Kennedy also criticized Nixon's policy of Vietnamization, which was the goal of having South Vietnamese forces take on more responsibility in combat. He said that the South Vietnamese government, now under the leadership of General Nguyen Van Thieu, needed to take even more responsibility for their country's rule.

On October 15, 1969, millions of Americans across the country demonstrated on Moratorium Day. They stayed home from jobs and classes to denounce the war. In many major cit-

Kennedy addressing a crowd on Moratorium Day. *(Courtesy of AP Images)*

ies, public officeholders addressed the peaceful protesters; in Boston, Kennedy addressed a crowd of nearly 100,000 people. He declared the need for ground troops to be pulled out completely from Vietnam within a year, and for naval and air support to be withdrawn by 1972.

On November 18, 1969, Kennedy's family suffered another blow when Joseph Kennedy passed away after suffering a heart attack. During Joseph's last night, Kennedy had comforted his father by sleeping next to his bed in a sleeping bag. Joseph Patrick Kennedy was eighty-one years old. His funeral, held on November 20, would have been Robert's forty-fourth birthday, and was three days before the six-year anniversary of John's assassination. Again Ted Kennedy delivered a eulogy for a close family member.

Ted Kennedy faced an election year in 1970, and his chances for a victory seemed uncertain. His election six years earlier had occurred right after John's assassination, and his image then was clean. Even at the beginning of 1969, Kennedy was so popular that many democrats were looking to him as a possible presidential candidate in the 1972 election. But his reputation had been tainted by the Chappaquiddick incident.

"The voters need reassurance," he told a reporter from the *New York Times*. "They need to see me, to be convinced that I'm reliable and mature. You can't counter the Chappaquiddick thing directly. The answer has to be implicit in what you are, what you stand for, and how they see you."

He tried to appeal to the diverse interests of his constituents. While campaigning he often woke early in the morning to meet with sanitation workers, policemen, and commuters on the subway. He traveled to schools, shopping plazas, retirement homes, coffeehouses, and public auditoriums, often making dozens of campaign stops every day.

Although Kennedy gave few formal speeches, he did continue to speak out against Vietnam. Another wave of anti-war protests had broken out and rocked the country in May of 1970. President Nixon had widened the unpopular war. Fearing communism would spread to Cambodia and Laos, two countries bordering Vietnam, Nixon ordered massive bombings. His actions appalled the world. Students across the United States protested violently. At Kent State University in Ohio, National Guardsmen opened fire on demonstrators, killing four students and wounding eleven others. Americans were horrified.

Although Kennedy talked about Vietnam, he also listened. During many of his informal stops on the campaign trail he spoke with his constituents and heard their needs. Those long days on the campaign trail aggravated Kennedy's fragile back. At the end of the day he often soaked in a warm bath, as his brothers had after long hours of campaigning. When not at home, he borrowed a friend's tub, and sometimes his aides even knocked on strangers' doors in search of a bathtub to ease his aching back.

Joan too made appearances, although her behavior was erratic. The campaign increased the strain on the couple's marriage, and her alcoholism worsened. She sometimes wore clothing that the press criticized as too short, too formal, or too revealing. Reporters noted that Ted and Joan Kennedy were not affectionate with each other in public. Both denied any troubles, though, stating that their marriage was strong.

The campaign proved difficult in other ways as well. The Kennedys were all too aware of the dangers of public life and campaigning. Running for political office made Kennedy highly visible. The family's fears of assassination were not unfounded. Kennedy received more death threats than anyone except the president, nearly two each week, and many serious enough for the Secret Service to investigate. Psychiatrists talked about the urge that mentally unstable people have to complete cycles of events, and fill out patterns, which would mean assassinating the third and last Kennedy brother.

Despite security and guards, no one felt safe. Police sharpshooters often stood at the ready when Kennedy marched in parades. Fearing a gunshot, Kennedy startled easily when a door slammed or even when a balloon popped. Joan was open with her fears for her husband's safety. Their eight-year-old son Teddy sometimes asked why his Uncle Bobby had been shot. At the end of each day on the campaign trail, Kennedy called his young son to assure him nothing bad had happened.

Kennedy spent months campaigning under intense pressure. In 1970 his bravery, determination, and tenacity paid off. In November, he clinched his reelection with 62 percent of the vote.

Although he won, his standing in the Senate remained the same. Between the impact of the Chappaquiddick scandal, the death of his father, and his reelection campaign, Ted Kennedy had been absent frequently from the Senate. Although he had served as the Whip since 1968, he had been unable to give the position his full attention. Now Senator Robert Byrd from West Virginia quietly amassed votes against Kennedy to challenge him for the job. In response, Kennedy approached senators for their support, phoning fifty-five of the fifty-seven Democratic senators in a twenty-four hour period, and calling them again the next day. But on January 22, 1971, Byrd defeated him for the position. It marked the first time Kennedy had been politically ousted by his own party. Although observers made much of the defeat, the detail-oriented job had pushed Kennedy away from the committee work that he excelled at and enjoyed. He shrugged off the defeat and continued working.

"I can't be bruised. I can't be hurt anymore," he told writer William Honan. "After what's happened to me, things like that just don't touch me."

Kennedy continued his focus on the Vietnam War. In 1972, Americans reelected President Nixon, who soon pushed for peace talks to end the war. Nixon also tried to improve ties with China and the Soviet Union. He hoped that a better relationship would prompt the two countries to persuade North Vietnam to cease the war. During the summer of 1972 serious negotiations continued between the United States and North Vietnam. On January 27, 1973, both sides signed the Paris Peace Accords, which ended American military involvement.

Next, Kennedy challenged the Nixon administration on a proposed military defense program. To prevent a possible Soviet attack, Nixon planned to install radar and missile systems in locations across the U.S. in order to shoot down potential incoming missiles. Kennedy led Congress in examining the costs of the installations being built and the technical feasibility of the proposal. He, like many senators, worried that such an action would spiral into an arms race, with the U.S. and the Soviet Union each stockpiling bigger and more effective weapons. As a result of the Vietnam War, Congress began taking a more critical approach when examining the president's military requests. Nixon's status further eroded when five men broke into the Democratic Party headquarters at the Watergate office building and were caught installing bugging equipment and cameras. In a complex chain of events, people learned that the president had authorized the criminal activity and had instructed his staff to cover up the incident. President Nixon began to undergo a criminal investigation.

In November of 1973, Kennedy's youngest son, Teddy, who was in seventh grade, discovered a small red lump under his knee. The family took Teddy to the hospital, where doctors discovered that the lump was a cancerous tumor. Worried about the spread of the cancer they decided to amputate Teddy's right leg.

The day of Teddy's surgery was the same day as Kennedy's niece's wedding. Kennedy had promised to give Robert's daughter Kathleen away during the ceremony. The church was located just a few blocks away from the hospital. That day, Kennedy rushed from the hospital, walked Kathleen down the aisle, spoke about Robert and the pride he would have felt, and then returned to the hospital.

Teddy's surgery went well. He began to use his artificial leg almost immediately afterwards. His father sent him a parade of visitors each day to entertain him during his hospital stay. But during the operation, doctors had discovered bone cancer cells, a more dangerous type of cancer. For the next two years Teddy would need to undergo chemotherapy, a relatively new type of chemical treatment in 1973. Every three weeks for six hours at a time he would receive shots of methotrexate, a strong drug that doctors hoped would kill the cancerous cells.

The treatment made him nauseated and sick, but like his father he was tough.

The 1970s were difficult years for the rest of Ted Kennedy's family as well. Joan had become more dependent on alcohol. She checked into Silver Hill, a rehabilitation facility in Connecticut, in order to try to defeat her addiction. After her release, she proudly told the media that she was now sober. Sadly, only one month later she was arrested for drunk driving and she returned to Silver Hill for more treatment. Articles about her alcoholism appeared in newspapers and magazines, along with gossip about her relationship with her husband.

All of Ted Kennedy's children also faced difficulties. Teddy continued to undergo his chemotherapy treatments. Kara, a student at the prestigious National Cathedral School in Washington, started running away from home. Patrick suffered from severe asthma. Kennedy also acted as a father to Robert's children, some of whom began to get into trouble, being caught with drugs and for speeding.

Amidst all of his personal family trouble, Ted Kennedy's supporters urged him to run for president in the 1976 election. Richard Nixon had resigned as president in August of 1974, under threat of impeachment. Upon his resignation, Nixon's vice president, Gerald Ford, had become president. Ford planned to run for reelection in 1976. Now The Citizens' Committee to Draft Ted Kennedy collected more than 30,000 signatures on petitions urging Kennedy to run as the Democratic candidate.

Kennedy weighed many factors. Teddy's cancer treatment had ended in 1975, six months ahead of schedule. Although the chemotherapy appeared to have defeated the cancer, the family feared a recurrence of the disease. He also worried that the campaign would put stress on Patrick, worsening his asthma. The pressure on Joan also would be intense, at a time when she needed rest and privacy.

Kennedy had suffered politically and personally in the last few years, with his brothers' assassinations, his near-fatal plane crash, and the Chappaquiddick scandal. Rumors about his own drinking and affairs with other women also hurt him. The threat of assassination continued to worry the family. After weighing all of the factors, Ted Kennedy made a firm announcement that he would not run for president in 1976.

"The uncertainties of higher office would place a great burden on my family," he said on television during an interview on *Meet the Press*.

In 1976, Kennedy did run for reelection to the Senate, though, and won another six-year term. That fall Democrat Jimmy Carter, a former peanut farmer who had become

Kennedy announces he will not run for president in 1976. *(Courtesy of AP Images)*

the governor of Georgia, faced Republican Gerald Ford for the presidency. Voters elected Carter as the next president of the United States, along with Walter Mondale as vice president.

Within a year after the election, Joan Kennedy left her husband and moved to the couple's apartment in Boston. For many years their marriage had been strained, and she decided they needed to live separately for a period of time. Joan had always faced difficulty fitting in with the competitive, ambitious, outgoing Kennedy clan. Now she left to concentrate on starting a new life, free of dependence on alcohol.

Joan began to attend a full-time graduate program at Lesley, a small teacher's college in Cambridge, Massachusetts. She took graduate classes in musical education. Within a few years, Joan would win acclaim for her narration during the Washington, D.C., National Symphony's performance of *Peter and the Wolf*; she would also continue to struggle with alcoholism.

During the Carter administration, Kennedy and the president often were at odds. They frequently disagreed over economic issues. While Carter was president, the American economy worsened. Inflation rates, or increases in prices, reached double digits. Interest rates on loans also went up. Oil

Kennedy speaking with President Carter (right) in 1976.

shortages forced more conservation, along with higher gasoline prices and rationing. Unemployment rates rose and the federal budget deficit increased to $66 billion. Carter worked hard to stop the economic slide, and though he succeeded in many ways, Kennedy often disliked the president's policies.

"President Carter likes to say he tackles the tough issues," Kennedy said. "Most of the time, he misses the tackles."

On November 4, 1979, tensions in the U.S. heightened when a hostage situation occurred in Iran. Mohammed Reza Pahlavi, the former shah, or leader, of Iran, had been a longtime ally of the United States, despite his autocratic rule. When revolution broke out in Iran, the shah was overthrown. The U.S. did not intervene, and the shah went into exile. Despite many refusals, Carter eventually allowed him to come into the United States to be treated for cancer. A group of Iranian militants, angry that the U.S. was sheltering the shah, seized the American embassy in the capital city of Tehran. They took nearly seventy Americans hostage. They demanded that Carter return the shah to Iran for trial, and that the U.S. issue an apology for supporting him, along with a promise not to further involve itself in Iranian affairs. Despite economic penalties and attempted military rescues, the hostages remained captive. Carter's handling of the crisis further eroded what little support and popularity he had.

As the 1980 presidential election approached, Kennedy needed to make a critical decision: challenge Jimmy Carter and run for president, or remain in the Senate. In 1968, his supporters had encouraged him to run immediately following Robert's assassination, but he was in mourning. In 1972, the Chappaquiddick incident plagued him. In 1976, family troubles kept him out of the race. Each time, though, Kennedy had hinted that he might run for president the next time around. Many considered it Kennedy's destiny to become president of the United States.

Ted Kennedy held discussions with family, friends, and staff to help make his decision. He also considered the stress on all of his family members, especially Joan. He and Joan met with her team of psychiatrists. Together, they decided the campaign could give her a positive goal on which to concentrate. Other factors gave him pause, though, such as his ability to win the race. He worried the Chappaquiddick scandal would return to haunt him, even though it had occurred ten years earlier. Knowing the risk of assassination, Kennedy spoke to the Secret Service about protection.

After weighing all of the factors, Ted Kennedy announced his candidacy on November 7, 1979, in front of Faneuil Hall in Boston. Faneuil Hall, built in the 1740s as a country market, was a Massachusetts landmark. Ted Kennedy had served his state for eighteen years. His announcement marked the beginning of the last presidential campaign for the Kennedy brothers.

six

Changing Directions

At first, polls showed Ted Kennedy as the favorite to win the Democratic nomination, making him the party's candidate in the November election. Soon after he officially announced his presidential campaign, though, he faced trouble. Especially problematic was a televised special on CBS entitled *Teddy*. During the program, Roger Mudd, a leading political reporter, questioned Kennedy about his reasons for running for president, his platform issues, and how he would contend with questions about the Chappaquiddick incident. Unable to give a clear reason why he wanted to be president, Kennedy gave vague references to his brothers and to leadership. He also evaded the Chappaquiddick issue. His rambling answers confused listeners and revived doubts some voters had about Kennedy.

Kennedy's first few weeks on the campaign trail were rocky. He had trouble stating his core positions. He also had difficulty explaining to voters how he differed from Jimmy Carter, a fellow Democrat. People expected him to be a dynamic presidential candidate, like John and Robert. Due to his family background and name, he received lots of media coverage, which actually worked against him. Small events, especially minor mistakes, turned into bigger stories and news spread fast. People chuckled when Kennedy referred to *"fam farmilies,"* instead of farm families, while campaigning in Iowa.

"His voice is strained, his timing is off, his eyes are glazed. Everything is wrong," wrote columnist Ellen Goodman.

The 1980 presidential campaign was hard on Kennedy's family. They fanned out across the country, making speeches, passing out flyers, and meeting voters. Despite Joan's own troubles, she rose to the occasion. She began giving interviews and appearing in public with her husband in a supportive role. The work helped her to stay sober. Kara and Teddy passed out leaflets, often enduring nasty comments about their father. Patrick flew back and forth to campaign stops with his father. On the airplane, the two played cards, talked, and discussed speeches. Twice, though, Patrick's asthma flared up so severely that the plane had to be diverted so he could be treated on the ground.

Kennedy's popularity with voters sank lower when Americans started to view Carter as a stronger leader. As the hostage crisis in Iran continued, Carter showed himself as tough and firm. He stuck to his principles, not giving into the militants' demands, but at the same time showing concern about the safety of the hostages and their return.

By the end of January 1980, Carter had taken the lead. In the Iowa primary on January 21, he received 59 percent of the vote, while Kennedy received only 31 percent. Despite

Kennedy being shown how to operate a combine during a 1979 presidential campaign stop in Marion, Iowa. *(Courtesy of AP Images)*

the troubling numbers in Iowa, Kennedy decided to continue on in the race.

In April, Kennedy made moves to rescue his campaign. To many voters, his presidential run had seemed halfhearted until now. He started to give strong speeches that highlighted the differences between him and Carter. He became clearer and more focused. But the changes and the revival came too late. Soon he had lost twenty-four out of thirty-four state primaries. Still he battled on until the Democratic National Convention, held in New York City in August. When it became clear he couldn't win, he conceded defeat on August 11, 1980.

The next day Jimmy Carter and his running mate Walter Mondale received the nomination of the Democratic Party. Although Kennedy and Carter had their many differences, Kennedy graciously supported him as the nominee and delivered an inspiring speech.

"For me, a few hours ago, this campaign came to an end," Kennedy said. "For all those whose cares have been our concern, the work goes on, the cause endures, the hope still lives, and the dream shall never die."

In the November election, Jimmy Carter lost the election to Republican Ronald Reagan, a former actor and popular governor of California. His running mate was the former Texas congressman, George H. W. Bush. In a landslide victory Reagan won the presidency, becoming the fortieth president of the United States. On January 19, 1981, successful negotiations secured the release of the American hostages in Iran, though the hostages were not formally released until the next day, just minutes after Reagan was sworn in as President. They had been held captive for 444 days.

Shortly after the campaign, in January of 1981, Joan and Ted Kennedy decided to divorce after twenty-two years of marriage. Their relationship had been rocky for many years. Her ongoing difficulties with alcohol and the frequent rumors of his affairs with other women had eroded their marriage. Their divorce went smoothly. They each had joint custody of their children. Kara and Edward were in college, and Patrick attended school at Fessenden in Boston, near his mother. Joan kept the apartment in Boston and the house on Cape Cod, while Kennedy continued living at their home near Washington.

Although he worried about his own reelection to the Senate in 1982 because of his loss in the presidential campaign, Kennedy again won his seat. His supporters around the country, though, continued to push for another presidential run. Only two years after his loss in 1980, rumors began swirling about another try. By November 1982 Kennedy was again the favorite for the Democratic presidential nomination, even though former Vice President Mondale would most likely enter the race as well. People readied themselves to line up supporters and start raising money for Kennedy's campaign.

At the time President Reagan's reelection seemed questionable. He looked vulnerable as the country had entered a recession, and unemployment rates were high. Also, in the recent elections, Democrats had won twenty-six seats formerly held by Republican congressmen. However, when the recession ended in 1983, Reagan's popularity soared. Defeating him in a presidential race began to look less certain.

Reporters believed that Kennedy truly had plans to run for president. Kennedy's own sister, Eunice, strongly advocated he run again in 1984. But Kennedy had reservations. The threat of an assassination was ever present. The demands of campaigning had also taken him away from his family and changed their lives. His children hadn't been immune to biting comments from some voters. Patrick's asthma also had worsened due to the stress of campaigning. In the end, Kennedy decided not to run again for family reasons. Instead, he focused on his work in the Senate.

Many people across the United States had turned their attention toward South Africa, a large nation in Africa that covers the southernmost section of the continent. The country is bordered by the Atlantic Ocean to the west and the Indian Ocean to the east. At the time, although 35 million black people lived in South Africa, the country's 5 million white people held all the political power. The South African government practiced a racial policy called apartheid to segregate the society by race. Apartheid officially began in 1948, but its roots ran deep. Decades earlier, white settlers had taken over the country and used racist policies to keep control of the government. Under apartheid, black and other nonwhite people could not vote, travel without permission, or own land, and they were forced to live in separate communities, obey a different set of laws, and work certain designated jobs.

In the 1950s, Nelson Mandela became president of a branch of the African National Congress, a political organization that tried to improve the lives of South Africa's black majority. A Johannesburg lawyer, Mandela was harassed by police and government officials, until finally in 1962 the South African government arrested him and sentenced him to five years in prison. But Mandela escaped, and remained on the run for more than a year. In 1964 he was again captured, and this time convicted of sabotage and treason, leading to a sentence of life imprisonment. He would remain in prison, still fighting against apartheid, for the next twenty-seven years. At times the apartheid government offered to free Mandela, but he refused until certain conditions were met and apartheid ended. Around the world, Mandela became a symbolic figure to all human rights activists. Mandela, like the Kennedys, believed that "One person can make a difference and everyone should try."

Many officials in the U.S. government, and students on numerous college campuses, pushed for the United States

Nelson Mandela *(Courtesy of AP Images/Richard Drew)*

to impose economic sanctions on South Africa. By refusing to trade with South Africa, Americans would be condemning the government's practices. Many nations frequently denounced apartheid, along with the growing violence in South Africa. President Reagan, however, supported maintaining trade with South Africa. He claimed that he hoped diplomatic and economic ties between the two countries would encourage reform.

Kennedy, hoping to learn more about the situation in South Africa, traveled to Johannesburg, the country's largest city. He was greeted by Reverend Desmond Tutu, a South African activist fighting apartheid; Tutu had won the Nobel Peace Prize for his work in South Africa. Kennedy traveled around South Africa, giving speeches and denouncing apartheid. In many areas he was met with protests and attacked in newspapers and on government-controlled television programming. He tried to meet with Nelson Mandela, but South African Foreign Minister Roelef Frederik "Pik" Botha denied his request. Instead, Kennedy visited with Winnie Mandela, his wife. She had been exiled and banned, meaning she was not allowed to meet with more than one person at a time, and her words could not be quoted in print.

Upon his return to the United States, Kennedy introduced a bill to the Senate. His bill would prohibit loans by U.S. banks to South African businesses, along with ending the sale of computers to the South African government. He also suggested banning the importation of krugerrands, a South African coin prized by collectors for its precious metal. Kennedy's bill was soon adopted. Within a year the Senate would pass a stronger bill condemning apartheid. Doing his part to fight apartheid

Kennedy speaks to reporters to raise awareness about the Free South Africa Movement in 1985. *(Courtesy of AP Images/John Duricka)*

only strengthened Kennedy's convictions to continue fighting for civil rights in countries around the world.

In December of 1984, Kennedy and his children Kara and Teddy traveled to Ethiopia, a country in eastern Africa, to bring attention to an ongoing famine. They witnessed the famine and food shortages that would kill more than 1 million Ethiopians. They toured stations set up to distribute food, and they helped hand out meals.

As a Kennedy, he had the power to focus public attention on important issues. However, the public avidly followed his personal life too. In 1984, Kennedy's mother Rose had a stroke, which left her bedridden. Soon she passed the family's house in Hyannis Port on to him, the only remaining Kennedy son.

Soon another tragedy struck, when David Anthony Kennedy, Robert's fourth child, died of a drug overdose. Kennedy's own children struggled too. Patrick, a senior at Andover, a boarding school in Massachusetts, underwent rehabilitation at a facility in New Hampshire for his drug addiction in the spring of 1985. Although that fall he began to attend Georgetown University in Washington, he dropped out after only two weeks.

Despite his family problems, Kennedy's dedication to his work remained strong. In February of 1986 he traveled to the Soviet Union to meet with Mikhail Gorbachev, the country's leader. For years the United States and the Soviet Union had been involved in the Cold War, each amassing stockpiles of nuclear weapons in order to protect themselves if ever the other country launched a nuclear attack. Both

Kennedy meeting with Mikhail Gorbachev in 1986. *(Courtesy of AP Images/Boris Yurchenko)*

countries wanted the ability to defend itself from attack, and have the ability to strike back. Kennedy, along with many others, fought fiercely for nuclear disarmament. His family understood personally the results of weapons and war. President Reagan at the time had plans to develop a space-based nuclear defense program that would shoot down any incoming missiles. The costly program was nicknamed *Star Wars*. The Russians saw it as a major obstacle to disarmament, as it gave America first-launch capability. Kennedy attempted to negotiate further talks between Reagan and Gorbachev. Eventually the two leaders signed a pact termed START, for Strategic Arms Reduction Treaty. It would stop the countries from deploying more than 6,000 nuclear warheads.

Later that year, Tip O'Neill, a Massachusetts congressman, announced that he would not seek reelection in 1986. O'Neil had held the seat since 1952: before O'Neill, the seat had been John F. Kennedy's. Ted Kennedy encouraged his son Teddy to run for the congressional seat. Although politics ran deep in the Kennedy family, Teddy wasn't interested. His cousin Joe, Robert's oldest son, ran instead and was easily elected. He would hold the seat for the next twelve years.

In 1988, more questions about Kennedy running for president arose. Some of his aides and many reporters thought he might run. As the head of the Kennedy clan, he was deeply involved with his own children, his nephews, and his nieces, and family concerns again troubled him. Some of his children and nephews continued to have personal problems. Kennedy's own problems were worse. Reports of him drinking heavily circulated around Washington, along with rumors of rash behavior while drunk. It was not the time to run for president. Instead he announced that he would run for reelection to the Senate again.

"I know that this decision means that I may never by president," he said. "But the pursuit of the Presidency is not my life. Public service is. . . . The thing that matters most, the greatest difference we can make, is to speak out, to stand up to lead and to move this nation forward. For me at this time the right place is in the Senate."

Kennedy asked his two oldest children, Kara and Teddy, to run his senate campaign. At the same time, Patrick became the first of Kennedy's own children to begin a career in politics. He became a delegate from Rhode Island, pledged to support presidential candidate Michael Dukakis at the Democratic National Convention. However, Patrick soon began to have difficulty walking. Doctors admitted him to Massachusetts General Hospital, where they discovered a tumor on the base of his spine. After five hours of surgery they determined it was benign.

Determined and tenacious like his father, Patrick began investigating running for a seat in the Rhode Island House of Representative. When he decided to run, his parents and relatives helped him campaign. On September 14, Patrick won the seat. Within a few years, he would go on to serve in the U.S. House of Representatives as a congressman from Rhode Island.

"None of the victories I have ever had in my political life has meant so much as this one tonight," Kennedy said upon his son's victory.

In November, Ted Kennedy again won reelection to his own senate seat. For years he had used his position to

Kennedy's son, Patrick, being sworn in as a representative in the Rhode Island House of Representatives. *(Courtesy of AP Images/Peter Southwick)*

champion civil rights for all citizens. In August of 1988, he played a key role in passing the Americans with Disabilities Act, which prohibited discrimination in employment, transportation, and housing, against people with disabilities.

"Disabled citizens deserve the opportunity to work for a living, ride a bus, have access to public and commercial buildings, and do all the other things that the rest of us take for granted," Kennedy said on the Senate floor. "Mindless physical barriers and outdated social attitudes have made them second class citizens for too long. This legislation is a bill of rights for the disabled, and America will be a better and fairer nation because of it."

In other areas of the world, restrictive governments began to allow more freedoms to their citizens. In 1989, Frederik Willem de Klerk became president of South Africa. He planned sweeping reforms and hoped for a nonviolent transition to an apartheid-free South Africa. On February 11, 1990, he freed Nelson Mandela, symbolically toppling the apartheid government in South Africa. Soon after, F. W. de Klerk and Nelson Mandela received the Nobel Peace Prize. When Mandela attended a lunch at the John F. Kennedy Presidential Library and Museum, he spoke about how meaningful Kennedy's 1984 trip had been.

"It was indeed very frustrating to know that he was at the gates of the prison," Mandela said, "but was unable to come in to give the message of hope, of strength, which as a black prisoner in white South Africa, gave us a lot of strength and hope, and the feeling that we had millions behind us both in our struggle against apartheid but in our special situation in prison."

By the late 1980s tremendous change had also occurred in Eastern Europe. Soviet leader Mikhail Gorbachev believed his government needed to be reformed. Since World War II, huge sums of money had been spent on the military, as a part of the Cold War. This had led to economic troubles, including shortages of goods, fuel, clothing, and much more.

The terms *perestroika,* meaning restructuring, and *glasnost,* meaning openness, described Gorbachev's changes. He began to offer citizens more freedom, deciding that the communist system wasn't right if it needed to hold its people by force. He allowed elections for certain government officials and let countries in Eastern Europe choose their own government. Many countries formerly controlled by the Soviet Union announced their freedom. Within weeks Poland, Hungary, Romania, and Bulgaria had instituted more democratic governments.

These changes were most dramatic in Berlin, Germany. After World War II, Germany had been divided into two countries. The division ran through the city of Berlin, separating neighborhoods and families; the grocery store at the end of the block was now technically in another country. The Allied countries of Britain, France, and the United States controlled West Germany, while the Soviet Union ruled East Germany. The Allies saw West Germany as key to rebuilding Europe. They worked to create a strong economy and rebuild industry. The Soviets, however, feared that a powerful Germany would rise to wage another war. In order to keep East Germany weak, they exacted harsh payments. Tensions escalated as the Allies and the Soviet Union saw each other as a threat.

In 1961, to prevent East Germans from crossing into West Germany, the Soviet Union, under leader Nikita Khrushchev, built a wall in Berlin, complete with armed guards and watchtowers. John F. Kennedy, president at the time, visited the Berlin Wall on June 26, 1963, and gave a speech about communism.

"Freedom has many difficulties and democracy is not perfect," he said. "But we have never had to put up a wall to keep our people in. There are some who say that Communism is the wave of the future. Let them come to Berlin."

On November 9, 1989, the East German government announced that East Germans could travel to West Germany. Thousands of East Germans gathered at the wall, chanting and singing. They began to break apart large sections of the wall that had kept them apart for twenty-eight years. The Berlin Wall had long been a symbol of the Cold War. At last it had fallen. In 1990 East Germany and West Germany united. Ted Kennedy visited Berlin and saw the remains of the wall his brother had condemned. "All of us have watched in awe in recent weeks as a new spirit of liberty has swept across Eastern Europe," Kennedy said. "Nowhere do these changes have greater symbolism for America than in the city of Berlin. In a sense, the Cold War began here, and now it is ending here . . . I only wish that President Kennedy could have come here himself, to see this new day that is beginning." Nearby Kennedy lay two white lilies in remembrance of his slain brothers.

Despite their many losses, the Kennedy family had endured. In 1990 the Kennedys celebrated Rose's one-hundredth birthday. Nearly four hundred people attended the celebration, as she watched from her wheelchair. Other family events, both happy and sad, occurred. In September, Kennedy's daughter Kara was married. However, Steve Smith, Kennedy's brother-in-law who had married Jean, passed away from cancer. It was a tough loss for Kennedy. Smith had been

East Berliners pour through an opening in the Berlin War after its fall in 1989. *(Courtesy of AP Images)*

like an older brother. With difficulty, Kennedy delivered his eulogy.

Kennedy was an accomplished and eloquent speaker at weddings, birthday parties, and funerals. He also had become an impressive figure in the Senate. However, in Washington, rumors about his heavy drinking overshadowed his long list of achievements. In 1991, this reputation again caused him trouble.

In March, Kennedy traveled to Palm Beach, Florida, where he visited with Jean and her children. Late that night he, Patrick, and his nephew William Kennedy Smith went to a bar. Smith met a woman who claimed later that he sexually assaulted her. At first gossip spread that Ted Kennedy was the assailant. Although Smith quickly corrected the false rumor, and was later acquitted, the incident damaged Kennedy's reputation. Around the same time Joan was arrested for drunk driving, and Teddy entered an alcohol rehabilitation facility in Connecticut, two weeks after graduating from Yale University.

The distressing events deeply shook Ted. He began to drink more heavily and more often. Colleagues advised him to take better care of himself

"You are a great senator now," Orrin Hatch, a senator from Utah, sternly warned Kennedy. "But you could go down in history as one of the all-time great senators. To do that you have to grow up. And you really have to stop drinking."

Things were about to brighten for Kennedy, though. One evening, he attended a dinner with his old friends Edmund and Doris Reggie, who had campaigned for John in the 1950s. He enjoyed talking with their thirty-seven-year-old daughter Victoria. Soon Kennedy sent her flowers and invited her to

Kennedy and Victoria Reggie *(Courtesy of AP Images/Kathy Willens)*

dinner. Although Kennedy was twenty-two years older than Victoria, age was no matter. By September the two were dating seriously. They began having dinner together every night at her house. Kennedy enjoyed playing with her two children from her former marriage, five-year-old Caroline and eight-year-old Curran. On Halloween he took them trick-or-treating around the neighborhood. Many of Kennedy's friends noted that he seemed happier and was drinking less.

On January 13, 1992, Kennedy proposed to Victoria. On July 3 the two married in a small ceremony in Kennedy's home in Virginia. Afterwards they took a short honeymoon in Vermont. They soon returned to Washington and began their new life together.

seven
The King of the Hill

O ver the years people have followed the story of the Kennedys. Some even call them America's royal family. People know the tale of Joseph, the driven father who made his fortune, and Rose the intelligent, politically savvy mother. Their many children capture the imagination of the nation. Three of their sons—Joe, John, and Robert—each gave their lives for their country. Many images represent the renowned family, from pictures of the Kennedy home in Cape Cod to stoic Rose Kennedy, clothed in a black dress, during her sons' funerals.

On January 22, 1994, at 104 years old, Rose Kennedy passed away. Many of her surviving children, grandchildren, and great-grandchildren gathered to remember her, reminiscing and telling stories. She had outlived several of her children and grandchildren, along with John's wife Jackie, who had passed away a year earlier from cancer. All of that grief left a permanent mark.

"It has been said that time heals all wounds," Rose wrote in her memoir. "I don't agree. The wounds remain. Time . . . covers them with some scar tissue and the pain lessens, but it is never gone."

People lined the roads as her funeral procession traveled from Cape Cod to St. Stephen's church in Boston for her funeral service. Her death seemed to mark the end of an era, when the Kennedys dominated politics.

Later that year, Ted Kennedy faced his senate reelection. The incident at Palm Beach had scarred him, and it was a tough race. He ran against a much younger candidate—Mitt Romney, the head of an investment firm in Boston. Michael Kennedy, one of Robert's sons, served as his campaign manager. During the difficult race, friends of Kennedy volunteered and helped raise money for his campaign. His new wife Vicki proved an adept campaigner. In November, Kennedy scored a resounding win when male and female voters of all ages, income levels, and education elected him for another term in office.

For a few years Kennedy's life seemed unmarked by tragedy. Then in January of 1998, his nephew Michael was killed in a skiing accident in Colorado. A year later, two more family members lost their lives. The Kennedy family had gathered at Cape Cod for what should have been a joyous time. Robert's youngest child, Rory, was to be married at the family compound. John's son, John F. Kennedy Jr., and his wife Carolyn Bessette Kennedy were flying in from New Jersey when their plane crashed into the ocean, just off the coast of Martha's Vineyard. Again, in the face of sorrow, Ted Kennedy helped hold his family together.

"When things are going badly he is somebody who you can turn to," his nephew Joe said. "Our family had gone

Kennedy presiding over a senate hearing on health care reform in 1994. *(Courtesy of AP Images/John Duricka)*

through too many crises, too many sad times, as other families have. But every time it happens, he is that guy that people look to."

In the many times of triumph and tragedy, Kennedy has continued to work diligently in the Senate. For many years, his days have followed the same pattern. He rises early in his home near Washington, and then looks over the day's work before having breakfast with his family. He arrives at his office, from which he can see the Washington Monument towering in the distance and the white columns of the Lincoln Memorial. A sea of phone messages already awaits him. During the day, he holds meetings, sees visitors, and talks with aides. In the Senate chamber he sits at the same desk his brother John used. He leaves the office with a bulging briefcase, crammed so full of memos, letters, and papers that it can't be closed. Sometimes after dinner he holds more meetings at his house with advisers, and then opens up the overflowing briefcase and continues working.

Kennedy has proved himself to be a dedicated senator. Many of his colleagues, both Democrats and Republicans, agree on his thoughtfulness, compassion, good humor, and ability to empathize with others. Those traits extend to his private life as well. Supporting his children and fatherless nieces and nephews has long been a priority.

A leading senator of his time, his list of accomplishments as a legislator is long. From his maiden speech on the Senate floor to encourage the passage of President John Kennedy's civil rights bill and then to help abolish poll taxes, Ted Kennedy has long championed justice. He has shown an ongoing commitment to improving health care for many in the United States and around the world. The family tragedies he has suffered through have influenced his opinions on health care—from his sister Rosemary's disabilities, to his brothers' deaths, to his own rehabilitation from a plane crash, to his children's stays in hospitals. Most recently his daughter Kara was diagnosed and treated for lung cancer. His former wife, Joan, defeated breast cancer.

Although he grew up in a wealthy family, surrounded by luxury and privileges, Senator Kennedy has worked to improve the lives of the poor and oppressed. He also has played key roles in solving global issues, in Vietnam, South Africa, the Soviet Union, and many other nations.

Since his early years in the Senate, the world has changed radically. Like so many American, he mourned the loss of 3,000 people following the terrorist attack in New York City on September 11, 2001. As he challenged leaders during past wars, he has led the fight in Congress protesting the ongoing war in Iraq that began in 2003.

Today, family photos line the walls of his office, along with special mementos, such as the American flag that stood in the corner of the Oval Office when John was president. He is sur-rounded by images of his mother, father, brothers, sisters, his own children, nieces, and nephews.

Senator Kennedy's ability to carry on in the face of terri-ble personal loss amazes many people, especially those who work closely with him. One of his staff members once com-mented to writer William Honan, "Can you imagine what's

A 2006 photo of Kennedy in his senate office *(Courtesy of AP Images/Pablo Martinez Monsivais)*

been going on inside him? Can you imagine? Some day his autopsy is going to show some scars that no one—not even us—realized were there."

In 2006 Kennedy shared his love of the Senate and Washington with younger children when he wrote the book *My Senator and Me: A Dog's Eye View of Washington, D.C.* The book tells the story of Kennedy's dog Splash as he spends a day at work with Kennedy. That year Kennedy also published the book *America Back on Track*, writing about the problems America faces, and proposing reforms to meet those challenges.

On May 17, 2008, Kennedy was rushed to the hospital following a seizure. A few days later, doctors diagnosed him with a cancerous brain tumor, shocking the nation. His colleagues missed his thundering voice and jokes in the hallways, along with the sight of him hitting tennis balls to his dogs

Kennedy sits with several family members in the waiting room of the Massachusetts General Hospital after being diagnosed with a cancerous brain tumor. *(Courtesy of AP Images/Stephan Savoia)*

on Capitol Hill. Kennedy underwent a daring new surgery, in which he was kept awake while surgeons operated on his brain, so that he could speak to the doctors as they worked, and they would avoid causing any permanent brain damage. The tumor was successfully removed, and Kennedy began to undergo chemotherapy and radiation. Still, the type of cancer Kennedy was afflicted with often proves to be fatal. However, early in July he returned to the Senate to cast his vote supporting a health care program. When he entered the senate floor with his son Patrick, his fellow senators broke out in applause.

Just a little more than a month later, Kennedy was scheduled to speak at the Democratic National Convention in Denver, Colorado, on August 25, 2008. His speech was supposed to provide an emotional opening to the convention, which would make history by nominating Barack Obama, the first African American candidate running for president in a major party. But in the days leading up to the convention, it was unclear whether or not Kennedy would be able to proceed.

Not only was he still in recovery from his brain surgery and chemotherapy, but forty-eight hours before the convention, Kennedy was afflicted with painful kidney stones as he arrived in Denver. He was relegated to a hospital bed in great pain, and it looked as though he might not be able to give the speech he'd pledged to make after coming out of his brain surgery. However, just two hours before he was due on stage, Kennedy told his wife and doctors that he was going to speak.

Kennedy was driven to the convention center, and a golf cart transported him and his doctors inside. A video tribute played, showing Kennedy's career and family, and he was introduced by Caroline Kennedy, his brother John's daughter. He took the stage at the convention to massive applause, an emotional moment of triumph for the senator who had been through so much and served so long. He gave his speech then, looking back at his legacy, but also promising to move forward into the future:

> I have come here tonight to stand with you to change America, to restore its future, to rise to our best ideals . . . As I look ahead, I am strengthened by family and friendship. So many of you have been with me in the happiest days and the hardest days. Together we have known success and seen setbacks, victory and defeat. But we have never lost our belief that we are all called to a better country and a newer world. And I pledge to you—I pledge to you that I will be there next January on the floor of the United States Senate when we begin the great test. . . . And this November, the torch will be passed again to a new generation of Americans . . . The work begins anew. The hope rises again. And the dream lives on.

Many commentators considered Kennedy's speech one of the most moving moments of the convention, and it showed again that Ted Kennedy was not merely President John F. Kennedy's youngest brother, the baby of a great American political family, but an important Washington icon in his own right. He has served as the senator from Massachusetts since 1962—more than four decades. During that time he has served under nine different presidents. Under fellow Democrat Bill Clinton, Kennedy saw many of his lifelong causes addressed. Later he saw former President George H. W. Bush's son become president, and Kennedy was often critical of that administration.

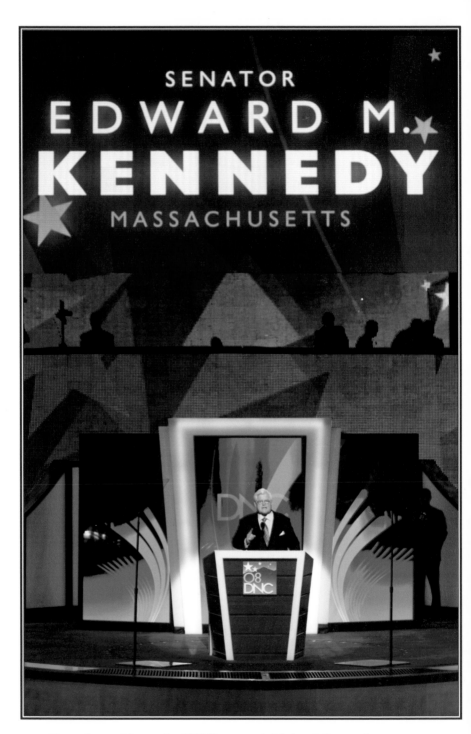

Kennedy speaking at the 2008 Democratic National Convention.
(Courtesy of AP Images/Ron Edmonds)

When it became clear that Obama would likely win the election, Kennedy repeatedly said that he wanted to be present at the inauguration. After a lifetime of fighting for civil rights, he was determined to be present at this historic moment.

On Inauguration Day, January 20, 2009, Kennedy got his wish, and was present while Obama took the oath of office. Later, though, at the celebratory luncheon that followed the ceremony, Kennedy suffered a seizure. He was quickly taken to the hospital and treated, where doctors, after testing, reported that the attack was most likely brought on by fatigue.

Though the excitement of the Inauguration undoubtedly played a role in Kennedy's seizure, his friends and family are sure the senator has no regrets. "He's a person who really does love history," said Senator Orrin Hatch, who helped escort Kennedy to the ambulance after the seizure. "He wouldn't miss this for the world."

Wise in the workings of the Senate, Kennedy is known as the King of the Hill. "Always the liberal lion, he has proven to be a courageous battler on the cutting edge of issues both domestic and foreign, maintaining the liberal tradition of his brothers, even when others in the Democratic Party showed less courage," said Ted Sorenson, John F. Kennedy's speechwriter. "Jack [John] and Bobby would have been proud."

Timeline

1932	Born February 22 in Bronxville, New York.
1938	Moves to London, England, with family when father, Joseph, becomes ambassador.
1941	Brothers Joe and John enlist to fight in World War II.
1943	Brother John becomes war hero when his boat, PT 109, sinks.
1944	Brother Joe dies during bombing mission.
1948	Sister Kathleen dies in plane crash in May.
1950	Enters Harvard University.
1951	Expelled from Harvard for cheating; enlists in the Army.
1953	Discharged from Army; begins attending Harvard again.
1958	Marries Joan Bennett.
1959	Receives law degree from University of

Virginia; begins working on John's presidential campaign.

1960   Daughter Kara Anne Kennedy born February 27; John elected president on November 8; Robert becomes attorney general.

1961   Son Edward Moore Kennedy Jr. born on September 26.

1962   Elected to U.S. Senate on November 6.

1963   Son Patrick Joseph Kennedy born on July 14; President John F. Kennedy assassinated on November 22.

1964   Makes first speech in Senate to help pass Civil Rights bill; suffers a near-fatal plane crash; reelected to Senate; Robert becomes senator.

1968   Dr. Martin Luther King Jr. assassinated; Robert runs for president; Robert assassinated on June 5.

1969   Chappaquiddick incident occurs in July; father Joseph dies.

1970   Reelected to the Senate; speaks out condemning the Vietnam War.

1976   Reelected to the Senate.

1980   Runs for president; loses nomination to Jimmy Carter.

1981	Divorces Joan.
1982	Reelected to the Senate.
1988	Reelected to the Senate; plays role in passing the Americans with Disabilities Act.
1992	Marries Victoria Reggie.
1994	Reelected to the Senate; mother Rose dies.
2000	Reelected to the Senate.
2006	Reelected to the Senate; publishes *My Senator and Me: A Dog's Eye View of Washington* and *America Back on Track*.
2008	Diagnosed with a cancerous brain tumor in May; undergoes treatment; speaks at Democratic National Convention.
2009	Atttends Barack Obama's Inaugural; suffers seizure from fatigue at Inaugural luncheon.

Sources

CHAPTER ONE: The Youngest Kennedy

p. 12, "No Irish Need Apply," Ted Kennedy, *America Back on Track* (New York: Viking, 2006), 4.

p. 15, "We don't want . . ." Adam Clymer, *Edward M. Kennedy: A Biography* (New York: Morrow, 1999), 13.

p. 19, "It is really terrible . . ." James MacGregor Burns, *Edward Kennedy and the Camelot Legacy* (New York: W. W. Norton & Company, 1976), 332.

p. 23, "He seemed to . . ." Kennedy, *America Back on Track,* 3.

p. 25, "He would have . . ." Joe McGinnis, *The Last Brother* (New York: Simon & Schuster, 1993), 188.

p. 27, "It's good that . . ." Kennedy, *America Back on Track,* 5.

CHAPTER TWO: Finding His Way

p. 38, "Fervent admirers . . ." Alfred Steinberg, *The Kennedy Brothers* (New York: G. P. Putnam's Sons, 1969), 199.

p. 39, "Here's to . . ." Clymer, *Edward M. Kennedy: A Biography,* 26-27.

p. 42, "Let every nation . . ." Burns, *Edward Kennedy and the Camelot Legacy,* 73.

CHAPTER THREE: The Three Brothers

p. 47, "One Kennedy is . . ." Burns, *Edward Kennedy and the Camelot Legacy,* 79.

p. 47, "Teddy Kennedy seeks . . ." Clymer, *Edward M. Kennedy: A Biography,* 37.

p. 50, "I ask . . ." McGinnis, *The Last Brother,* 306.

p. 53, "now and . . ." Diane McWhorter, *A Dream of Freedom: The Civil Rights Movement From 1954-1968* (New York: Scholastic, 2004), 72.

p. 54, "Governor, you are . . ." Ibid, 72.

p. 60, "A freshman senator . . ." McGinnis, *The Last Brother,* 360.

p. 60, "My brother was . . ." Ibid, 360.

p. 63, "I never thought . . ." Clymer, *Edward M. Kennedy: A Biography,* 64.

CHAPTER FOUR: The Last Brother

p. 66, "It is wrong . . ." McWhorter, *A Dream of Freedom: The Civil Rights Movement From 1954-1968*, 119.

p. 66, "There is no . . ." Clymer, *Edward M. Kennedy: A Biography,* 66.

p. 76, "I have such . . ." Ibid, 109.

p. 78, "Let us dedicate . . ." Ibid, 111.

p. 78, "I Have a Dream . . ." McWhorter, *A Dream of Freedom: The Civil Rights Movement From 1954-1968*, 94.

p. 78, "He will never . . ." Clymer, *Edward M. Kennedy: A Biography*, 111.

p. 80, "sort of leaning . . ." Ibid, 114.

p. 80, "a good and decent . . ." Steinberg, *The Kennedy Brothers,* 183.

p. 80, "As he said . . ." Clymer, *Edward M. Kennedy: A Biography,* 119.

p. 82, "Over the last . . ." Ibid, 121.

p. 82-83, "Like my brothers . . ." Ibid.

p. 84, "I like to walk . . ." Burns, *Edward Kennedy and the Camelot Legacy,* 177-178.

CHAPTER FIVE: Scandal and Sorrow

p. 88, "I was overcome . . ." William Honan, *Ted Kennedy: Profile of a Survivor* (New York: Quadrangle Books, 1972), 84.

p. 92, "The voters need . . ." Clymer, *Edward M. Kennedy: A Biography,* 169.

p. 95, "I can't be bruised . . ." Honan, *Ted Kennedy: Profile of a Survivor,* 5.

p. 98, "The uncertainties of . . ." Clymer, *Edward M. Kennedy: A Biography,* 169.

p. 100, "President Carter . . ." Ibid, 294.

CHAPTER SIX: Changing Directions

p. 103, *"fam farmilies,"* Clymer, *Edward M. Kennedy: A Biography,* 294.

p. 103, "His voice is strained . . ." Lester David, *Good Ted, Bad Ted* (New York: Carol Publishing Group, 1993), 193.

p. 105, "For me . . ." James S. Robbins, "Clinton Campaign Reminiscent of 1980 Race," CBS News, May 13, 2008.

p. 107, "One person can . . ." Official Web site of the U.S. Senate, http://kennedy.senate.gov.

p. 113, "I know that this . . ." Clymer, *Edward M. Kennedy: A Biography,* 386.

p. 113, "None of the . . ." Ibid, 437.

p. 115, "Disabled citizens . . ." Ibid, 454.

p. 115, "It was indeed . . ." Ibid, 470.

p. 117, "Freedom has . . ." Ibid, 458.

p. 117, "All of us . . ." Ibid.

p. 119, "You are . . ." Lester. *Good Ted, Bad Ted,* 244.

CHAPTER SEVEN: The King of the Hill

p. 123, "It has been . . ." "Rose Fitzgerald Kennedy/1890-

1995—Matriarch Dies at 104 'She was the Most Beautiful Rose of All,'" *Seattle Times,* January 23, 1995.

p. 123-124, "When things are . . ." Clymer, *Edward M. Kennedy: A Biography,* 605.

p. 126-127, "Can you imagine . . ." Honan, *Ted Kennedy: Profile of a Survivor,* 4-5.

p. 129, "I have come here tonight . . ." Ted Kennedy, "Transcript: Edward Kennedy's DNC Speech," *CNN.com.*

p. 131, "He's a person who . . ." Michael Scherer, Jay Newton-Small, and Karen Tumulty, "Ted Kennedy Suffers Seizure at Inaugural," *Time.com,* January 20, 2009.

p. 131, "Always the liberal lion . . ." Tim Rutten, "Ted Kennedy, the Lion of the Senate," *Los Angeles Times,* May 21, 2008.

Bibliography

Barr, Roger. *The Vietnam War.* San Diego, CA: Lucent Books, 1991.

Burns, James MacGregor. *Edward Kennedy and the Camelot Legacy.* New York: W. W. Norton & Company, 1976.

Chellis, Marcia. *Living with the Kennedys.* New York: Simon & Schuster, 1985.

Clymer, Adam. *Edward M. Kennedy: A Biography.* New York: Morrow, 1999.

Collier, Christopher and James Lincoln Collier. *The U.S. and the Cold War 1945-1989.* New York: Benchmark Books, 2002.

David, Lester. *Good Ted, Bad Ted.* New York: Carol Publishing Group, 1993.

Gaines, Ann Graham. *Nelson Mandela and Apartheid in World History.* Berkeley Heights, NJ: Enslow Publishers, 2001.

Honan, William. *Ted Kennedy: Profile of a Survivor.* New York: Quadrangle Books, 1972.

Keeley, Jennifer. *The Cold War: Containing the Communists, America's Foreign Entanglement.* New York: Lucent Books, 2003.

Kennedy, Edward Moore. *America Back on Track.* New York: Viking, 2006.

Lerner, Max. *Ted and the Kennedy Legend.* New York: St. Martin's Press, 1980.

Lippman, Theo, Jr. *Senator Ted Kennedy: The Career Behind the Image.* New York: W. W. Norton & Company, 1976.

Marchione, Marilynn. "Experts: Experimental Meds an Option for Kennedy." *Chicago Tribune,* June 9, 2008. http://www.chicagotribune.com.

McGinnis, Joe. *The Last Brother.* New York: Simon & Schuster, 1993.

McWhorter, Diane. *Dream of Freedom: The Civil Rights Movement From 1954-1968.* New York: Scholastic, 2004.

Miga, Andrew. "Kennedy Undergoing Surgery for Brain Tumor." Yahoo News, June 2, 2008. http://www.yahoo news.com.

Official Web site of Ted Kennedy. http://www.kennedy. senate.gov.

Official Website of the U.S. Senate. http://kennedy. senate.gov.

Robbins, James S. "Clinton Campaign Reminiscent of 1980 Race." CBS News, May 13, 2008. http://www. cbsnews.com.

Rutten, Tim. "Ted Kennedy, the Lion of the Senate." *Los Angeles Times,* May 21, 2008.

Seattle Times News Services. "Rose Fitzgerald Kennedy/ 1890-1995—Matriarch Dies at 104—'She was the Most Beautiful Rose of All.'" *Seattle Times,* January 23, 1995.

Scherer, Michael, Jay Newton-Small, and Karen Tumulty. "Ted Kennedy Suffers Seizure at Inaugural." *Time.com,* Januray 20, 2009.

Sherrill, Robert. *The Last Kennedy.* New York: The Dial Press, 1976.

Steinberg, Alfred. *The Kennedy Brothers.* New York: G. P. Putnam's Sons, 1969.

Wilborn, Hampton. *Kennedy Assassinated! The World Mourns: A Reporter's Story.* Cambridge, MA: Candlewick Press, 1997.

Web sites

http://www.kennedy.senate.gov
Ted Kennedy's official Senate Web site provides a general background, along with descriptions of the senator's position on many issues and his past achievements.

http://www.whitehouse.gov
Readers interested in learning more about the government can find information on this site, as well as take virtual tours of the White House and test themselves with trivia.

http://www.jfklibrary.org
The Web site of John F. Kennedy Presidential Library and Museum offers detailed biographies of each of the members of the Kennedy family.

Index

DATE DUE